HENRY O'NEILL OF THE 'CELTIC CROSS'

Frontispiece—Henry O'Neill's *Self-portrait*, showing the artist probably in his 60s. Courtesy of the National Library of Ireland (No. 2293).

Henry O'Neill of the 'Celtic Cross'

Irish antiquarian artist and patriot

PETER HARBISON

Wordwell

For Harry McDowell,
O'Neill's champion.

First published in 2015
Wordwell Ltd
Unit 9, 78 Furze Road, Sandyford Industrial Estate, Dublin 18
www.wordwellbooks.com

Cover image—Signed view of *Luggala*, with Lough Tay in the background. Reproduced with the kind permission of the Hon. Garech Browne.

ISBN 1 905569 87 8

British Library Cataloguing-in-Publication Data.
A catalogue record for this book is available from the British Library.

Typeset in Ireland by Wordwell Ltd
Copy-editor: Emer Condit
Printed by Gráficas Castuera, Pamplona

The publisher acknowledges a generous grant from Harry McDowell towards the publication of this book.

CONTENTS

PERSONAL ACKNOWLEDGEMENTS

It is with great pleasure that I thank here first Henry McDowell, who asked me to write this book to honour the name of Henry O'Neill, a number of whose paintings he owns. But it would not have been possible to do that without the artist's sketch-books preserved in Glenstal Abbey, which its abbot, Dom Mark Patrick Hederman OSB, and its then librarian, Dr Colmán Ó Clabaigh OSB, kindly placed at my disposal for a long time, for which I would like to thank them both wholeheartedly. For permission to reproduce the artist's works in their care I would like to thank Honora Faul and Glenn Dunne of the National Library of Ireland, Anne Hodge, Maria McFeely and Louise Morgan of the National Gallery, Raghnall Ó Floinn, Sandra Heise and Finbar Connolly of the National Museum, Collins Barracks, and Brian Walsh of the Dundalk Museum. My thanks also go particularly to those private owners who have kindly allowed me to reproduce their O'Neill works here: the earl of Erne, the Hon. Garech Browne, Michael and Marianne Gorman, Cróine Magan and Dolores Treacy (with help from her son Enda). For help in obtaining pictorial material my thanks are due to David Britton and Marcia Kenna-Colgan of James Adam's and Sons, Rhiannon Carey Bates, James Fennell, Siobhán FitzPatrick, Petra Schnabel and Dave McKeon of the Royal Irish Academy, Liam Gaynor of the Dundealgan Press, Bernard Meehan and Brian McGovern of Trinity College, Dublin, and Kathryn Eliza Milligan of TRIARC, as well as Dr Rachel Moss and Donal Fenlon of the Royal Society of Antiquaries of Ireland. Finally, I would like to thank the following who have been very helpful in one way or another in the preparation of this book: Arabella Bishop and Eliza McCormack of Sotheby's, Lesley Poggemoeller of the Ivey-Selkirk Gallery in St Louis, Missouri, Anne Brady of Vermilion, the photographer David Davison, Nicola Figgis of University College, Dublin, Jim and Thérèse Gorry of the Gorry Gallery, Helena King and Roisín Jones of the Royal Irish Academy, Clare Lanigan, Clemency Pleming of Oxford University, and Peter Rowan. Also thanks to Fidelma Slattery of the Royal Irish Academy for helpful comments on the presentation of the notebook extracts.

PHOTOGRAPHIC ACKNOWLEDGEMENTS

The National Gallery of Ireland: Frontispiece, Pls 13 and 14
The National Library of Ireland: Pl. 23, Figs 4, 8, 11, 13 and 42
The National Museum of Ireland: Pl. 15 (a–d)
Trinity College, Dublin: Fig. 10
The Royal Irish Academy: Fig. 9, Pls 1–4
James Adam's and Sons: Pl. 11
TRIARC: Fig. 5
James Fennell: Pls 7–11, 16 and 21–2
Brian McGovern: Pl. 20
Michael O'Dwyer, Kilkenny: Pl. 34

Fig. 1—Self-portrait of the young artist as he seeks inspiration in the midst of his hectic work (unnumbered page in Glenstal Sketch-book G).

Henry O'Neill is best known as an artist, archaeologist, publisher and polemicist, as seen through his various books—*The sculptured crosses of ancient Ireland*, *Ireland for the Irish* and *The round towers of Ireland* (County Dublin only). But they give a mere inkling of the impressive compendium of work that O'Neill did throughout a long and active career spanning 40 years and more. We find out a lot more through the sketch-books of his that survive, and realise what an incredible amount of travelling and sketching he did through his interest in castles or tower-houses, though he also covered a wide variety of other monuments, from prehistoric times almost up to his own day. These sketch-books and notebooks have fortunately been preserved in Glenstal Abbey, and it is thanks to the abbot, Dom Mark Patrick Hederman OSB, and Dr Colmán Ó Clabaigh OSB that I have had access to them and am in a position to reproduce some of their contents with permission.

On the inside back cover of the largest of these sketch-books, a large folio volume bearing the simple title 'Antiquities', O'Neill pasted in a small sheet of paper bearing the following:

Book marked B
Do.   –   D
Do.   –   F
Do.   –   G
Do.   –   H
Do.   –   K
Quarto sketch book Castles bearing date 1849
Folio Book with some Manuscripts on Round
    Towers
Do. .... on Irish Castles
Collection reduced drawings Thos. O'Neill [son]
Seven lots folio Manuscript ready publication
Small 4to Book Manuscript drawings etc. Trim Castle
A pile of Loose Manuscript 4½ inches thick
9 sketch books
Large Folio Book Antiquities
Round Towers, Castles etc.

These are *exactly* what I now have.

With the exception of the last item ('Round Towers, Castles etc.'), the items listed above were ticked off in pencil, possibly by O'Neill himself. But, sad to relate, we are no longer in a position to tick off as many as he did, simply because a number of these notebooks are now untraceable. We should, however, count ourselves lucky that the Library of Glenstal Abbey does preserve a number of them:

B, marked 'Castles',
G, marked 'Round Towers' (though also covering
    castles),
K, technical terms and twenty castles in Tipperary and
    Cork,
'Folio Book on Irish Castles',
the large folio book marked 'Antiquities',

and a slim volume on round towers which may be the 'Folio book with some manuscripts on Round Towers', comprising Clondalkin, Glendalough, Taghadoe and Oughterard (Co. Kildare), and a table of 'Doorways of Towers'.

It would be wonderful if the other items now lost—particularly the seven lots of folio drawings ready for publication—ever turned up, kept intact perhaps in some neglected attic, but for the moment we must be thankful for the material that we know to have survived.

Pasted onto the inside front cover of the large folio volume of 'Antiquities' is a flyer of Carson Brothers of 7 Grafton Street, Dublin, offering for sale (with privilege to republish), 'for the moderate sum of One Hundred Pounds',

The O'Neill Manuscripts

This unique collection comprises … his unpublished History of the Castles of Ireland, Irish Antiquities, etc. They are invaluable as a record of Irish History and Archaeology, and are comprised of the following lots.

It goes on to list the Glenstal material outlined above, and gives more details of some of the untraced material:

Book marked B medium 4to, Contains Pencil and Pen-and-Ink Drawings of Castles, and their Measurements, Descriptions, Newspaper Cuttings, Letters, and Photographs bearing on that Subject and Antiquities.

Book marked D—Descriptions, Measurements and Drawings.

Book E *which has been struck out and marked* Lost.

Book F *described as* Descriptions, Measurements and Drawing.

Book G, in folio, Round Towers, Castles, Cromlechs &c, with Newspaper Cuttings, Descriptions, Drawings, and Measurements.

H, in folio, with Drawings, Measurements, and Cuttings, Description of Antiquities, Round Towers, Notes and Criticisms.

K, medium 4to, with Drawings, Measurements, and Descriptions of Castles &c.

A Quarto sketch book of Castles, some bearing date 1849.

A [*Folio crossed out—4to inserted by hand*] book with some Manuscripts on Round Towers.

D(itt)o [*crossed out and Folio inserted by hand*] book on Irish Castles.

A Collection of reduced drawings (Pen-and-Ink) of Castles copied from the foregoing suitable for publication. By Thomas O'Neill.

Seven lots of folio manuscript of Irish castles &c., prepared and ready for publication. By the late author.

A small 4to book, partially filled with Manuscript, Drawings, and Description of Trim Castle &c.

A Lot of manuscripts of Irish Castles, Antiquities, Antiquarian Notes, &c., 6½ inches thick.

Seventeen [*crossed out, and seemingly replaced by nine*] Sketch and Note Books, nearly all filled with Drawings, Measurements and Descriptions of Castles, Towers, and Antiquities &c.

Large Folio Book—*identical with the large folio volume marked 'Antiquities' mentioned above.*

In a final note, W.A. Hinch, the vendor, says that

The drawings are therefore unique records of the past, as, in consequence of natural decay, and worse, the vandalism and wanton destruction (which had to be interdicted and restrained by Act of Parliament) of those landmarks of Irish History by the agricultural

Fig. 2—*Kilcrea Castle, Co. Cork*, with remains of the Franciscan friary and the bridge over the River Bride (Glenstal Sketch-book K, p. 63).

portion of the community, these historic monuments of the past have, in a vast number of instances, disappeared—this, therefore, renders the O'Neill collection of inestimable value.

This Carson Brothers sale flyer is undated, though mention of 'the late author' suggests its date as being around the late nineteenth century or *c.* 1900. It shows, however, that many missing items were still available and kept together at the time, along with what survives. What has happened to these lost items we may never know but, with any luck, they may still turn up.

Among the manuscript books, a torn piece of paper bears on one side the printed heading *The Irish Ecclesiastical Record (Publishers: Browne and Nolan, Limited, Dublin)*, the address of The Cellarer, Glenstal Priory, Murroe, Co. Limerick, and the postal stamp of 1948. On the other side we find the words 'The Manuscripts on Irish Antiquities compiled in the middle of the XIXth century by H. O'Neill and purchased by Vincent Scully' (a name recurring in at least three generations of this Tipperary family and therefore difficult to identify precisely). It was possibly from this Vincent Scully, or one of his descendants, that Glenstal

may have bought or inherited the O'Neill material.

Obviously the lost material would have been able (and will be able, if ever located) to fill in the gaps in O'Neill's career which are all too evident in the present volume. The book with some drawings bearing the date 1849 would, for instance, have been particularly relevant in providing us with an insight into O'Neill's activities after he returned home from an unfortunate, not to say disastrous, sojourn with the British army around 1847–8. The item marked K would, at least, seem to give us the sequel. Other than one starting with a glossary of technical terms which he intended to use, most of O'Neill's sketch-books and notebooks are taken up with sketches, plans and descriptions, very detailed but often tedious, of various castles, beginning with those which he encountered in counties Tipperary and Cork. These he covered in the first half of the year 1851, starting on 5 January, as if he were determined to turn over a new leaf in the second half of the nineteenth century. His pen sketches in blue ink are charming and often atmospheric, but here lack of space forces us to make a selection from among the best of them. Nor is it intended in the text to go into detail on each of the castles visited. The lost sketch-books would doubtless have provided us with even more castles which O'Neill would have visited in Munster (and doubtless elsewhere as well), but it is unlikely that he would have seen all of the castles in County Cork. O'Neill subsequently sketched castles in Kilkenny and Dublin and, when he moved to Dundalk in the 1860s, he made drawings of many tower-houses in Louth and surrounding counties.

It might be mentioned that O'Neill's interests were not entirely confined to castles, as he also sketched other classes of monuments, from the Early Christian pillar stone at Kilnasaggart, Co. Armagh (Fig. 3), to an inscribed plaque of 1674 inserted into a bridge in Dundalk. Medieval abbeys, however, were not his forte, as we can see when he visited Kilcrea Castle in County Cork[1] and virtually ignored the much more important Kilcrea Abbey close by (Fig. 2). We do know, however, that he went out of his way to visit Creevelea Friary, near Dromahaire, Co. Leitrim,[2] and we should make no value judgements on what types of monuments, or even individual monuments, he may or may not have visited, as these may have been contained in the many notebooks which have been lost.

NOTES
1. Sketch-book K, pages 63–72.
2. Sketch-book B 2.

Fig. 3—Inscribed pillar stone at *Kilnasaggart, Co. Armagh* (Glenstal Sketch-book B, p. 45).

1

INTRODUCTION

The name Henry O'Neill has been largely airbrushed out of Ireland's antiquarian story because he came off second best to his great adversary George Petrie in the controversy about Irish round towers which raged throughout much of the nineteenth century. O'Neill was convinced that they were of pagan origin, whereas Petrie argued correctly in favour of their Christian associations. Nevertheless, even if he failed in academic argument, O'Neill must—along with Petrie, G.V. Du Noyer and W.F. Wakeman—be ranked very highly among Irish antiquarian *artists* of the late Georgian and Victorian periods, hence the need to restore his reputation in this volume.

Petrie has had a champion in Peter Murray, Director of the Crawford Gallery in Cork,[1] and Du Noyer's work has been highlighted by Petra Coffey[2] and Fionnuala Croke,[3] but so far no one has come forward to plead the cause—and value—of Henry O'Neill, who has almost fallen into oblivion because of his rejected round tower theories. As we shall see, however, he made a major impact in encouraging interest in Ireland's great high crosses, and would have written the first major book on Irish castles had death not cut short his intentions.

It should be pointed out at the very start that there is a danger that credit for his work could all too easily be given to others, as there were people of a similar name among his contemporaries. One of these was a Young Irelander—Charles Henry O'Neill—referred to in an article by Owen Dudley Edwards[4] as having been mentioned by Gavan Duffy in his work on the Movement, but he could more easily be confused with the Henry O'Neil[5] who had only one 'l' in his name, an artist of historical tableaux, portraits and landscape paintings who died in the same year as our

Henry O'Neill, 1880, the former on 18 March, the latter on 21 December.

According to the *Irish Builder* of 1 April 1880, O'Neil was born in St Petersburg, but our Henry O'Neill was of Irish birth, though there are conflicting views as to precisely when and where he was born. The usually reliable W.G. Strickland[6] has Clonmel, Co. Tipperary, as his native heath, and the year of his birth as 1798. A recent Eamonn de Burca catalogue[7] gives Dundalk as his birthplace, while in a preliminary flyer for *The ancient high crosses of Ireland* (of which the Royal Irish Academy preserves a copy in the Windele Collection) he styles himself H. O'Neill (of Kilkenny), though that is more likely to be merely an indication of where he was living at the time. In his obituary in the *Irish Builder* of 1 January 1881, he is given as being 80 years old when he died, which would have made him of equal age with the century. The *Athenaeum* of 1 January 1881 said that he had reached the age of 81, having attained a considerable excellence in delineating ancient Irish artwork in many of its delicate and characteristic forms. But because, as we shall see (p. 90), he said himself in 1877 that he was verging on 80 years of age, we may take it that 1798 is the most likely year of his birth.

We are again indebted to Strickland for details of his childhood and early life, though sadly the author of that splendid *Dictionary of Irish artists* (1913) does not supply us with the source of his information. Strickland tells us, anyway, that O'Neill was an only child, named after his father, and the son of a daughter of Samuel Watson, a bookseller and publisher of *The Gentleman's and Citizen's Almanac*. Both of his parents died while he was young, and his upbringing and education were taken over by his aunt,

Sarah O'Neill, who owned a haberdashery in Dublin's South Great George's Street. There he apparently helped out with patterns for her shawl and lace but, owing to a disagreement with her, he left her and was taken up by his mother's family.

O'Neill's talent for drawing manifested itself early, and in 1815 he became a pupil of the Dublin Society Schools and was awarded first prize for every category for which he entered—Figure Drawing, Landscape and Ornament Drawing, according to Gitta Willemson,[8] who added his attendance at the School of Modelling in 1816. She lists, further, premiums for him in the three years 1820–2. Strickland quotes the Dublin Society as presenting O'Neill with a silver medal 'as a reward of his industry and talent' in having produced several drawings from the living figure— probably the same medal mentioned by Willemson under the year 1825. It must have been around this time that he was employed by William Allen, the print-seller in Dublin's Dame Street and author of *Allen's elementary drawing book*. As Nicola Figgis kindly pointed out to me, O'Neill went on himself to publish a more detailed version entitled *A guide to pictorial art. How to use black lead pencil, chalks, and water colours, the capabilities of these materials, with every information necessary to put the student on the proper course for attaining excellence in the fine arts.* The title adequately explains the content of this volume of more than 90 pages, which was published by Rowney, Dillon and Rowney in London in 1846. A copy of this extremely rare work is known to be preserved in the Bodleian Library in Oxford. In the Preface, O'Neill argues that he had acquired an accurate knowledge of what a student in art would require to know from a master, 'having had much experience in teaching drawing … both in his former career as a teacher, and in his present one as an artist'. We know of at least one teaching role he undertook when, as an alumnus of the Dublin Society's Drawing Schools in 1836, he offered 'to deliver to the Pupils at present in the Schools, after the usual school hours, a short course of lectures in Perspective, gratuitously'[9] — a proposal supported by the well-known painter Martin Cregan, who was president of the Royal Hibernian Academy at the time.

The previous year, 1835, when living in the appropriately named Harry Street, O'Neill exhibited his works for the first of many times with the Royal Hibernian Academy of Arts. One of these may have been the landscape offered by the Cynthia O'Connor Gallery in March–April 1985. The titles of his paintings exhibited then and in subsequent years are too long to be given here (they are listed in the Appendix, pp 101–5), but it may be mentioned that in his view of Clondalkin, Co. Dublin, he demonstrated publicly for the first time his fascination with round towers, a subject which continued to attract him for the rest of his life. Otherwise, all of the watercolour scenes he exhibited were landscapes in County Wicklow, including a scattering of ancient monuments, as exemplified by his 'View of the Seven Churches, Glendalough, Co. Wicklow'. Like most of the watercolours O'Neill is recorded as having exhibited during his lifetime, almost all of them have dropped out of sight, only very few having come into public ownership, though at least a small number are known to have been preserved in private collections. Perhaps the appearance of this volume will help to bring some more to light.

In the case of County Wicklow, however, we at least have survivors of his work there in the aquatints of his drawings which appeared in the book *Picturesque sketches of some of the finest landscape and coast scenery of Ireland from drawings by G. Petrie, R.H.A., Andrew Nicholl, and H. O'Neill*, Vol. 1, published in Dublin by Wakeman in 1835. It was reissued in 1843,[10] and O'Neill's watercolours were also reproduced in thirteen out of the fourteen coloured aquatints in *Fourteen views in the County of Wicklow, from original drawings by H. O'Neill and A. Nicholl*, published that same year by Wakeman in Dublin and Ackermann in London.[11] This seems to have been the only time that Petrie and O'Neill were intended to appear together in print (hopefully amicably) before O'Neill began to disagree openly with Petrie. One may wonder whether the enmity may have stemmed from O'Neill's jealousy, after a reviewer on page 609 of the *Dublin University Review* of May 1835 criticised O'Neill and praised Petrie in the following passage, reviewing the first part of the work that was issued:

We promise ourselves a rich treat in the subsequent

4   HENRY O'NEILL OF THE 'CELTIC CROSS'

parts. We have as yet nothing from the pencil of George Petrie, and in the advertisement of the second part, we do not see the mention of his name—why is this? Surely even in the four drawings already engraved, there were subjects worthy of his genius and taste. Why did he not undertake the Vale of Ovoca, and prevent that exquisite subject from being spoiled?— and spoiled it has been, with all due deference to Mr. O'Neill. Ireland is proud of Petrie, and we will not be satisfied, unless, in a very early number, we see something from his pencil—some illustration in which his genius shall lend, if possible, additional enchantment to the scene that he portrays.

It must be said, however, that O'Neill's coloured lithographs of Wicklow published in the *Picturesque sketches* tend to be stiff and stylised, though the human figures represented do nevertheless appeal, as seen, for instance, in those having a picnic beside a waterfall in the scene on the Dargle opposite page 13. He uses strong colours in the lithographs, as can be seen in the good examples illustrated here (Pls 1–3).

O'Neill continued to exhibit almost every year at the Royal Hibernian Academy until 1847 but, like a roving and unsettled spirit, changing his Dublin address almost annually—39 Great Brunswick Street (now Pearse Street) in 1838, North Earl Street in 1840, Trinity College (where he may have worked briefly for a period) in 1841, and 5 St Andrew's Street in 1842–7, though with a gap in 1845 and 1846 (the height of the Famine), when he had moved to lodgings near the Grand Canal by 1847.

By then, however, his relationship with the Royal Hibernian Academy had changed temporarily for the worse. He had been elected an Associate of the Academy in May 1837. Six years later a vacancy occurred in the full Membership, but it took a long time to fill because, it was alleged, there was some want of merit among the Associates. Not for the last time in his life, O'Neill felt aggrieved and, in the following January, he resigned on the pretext that someone more worthy might be elected. Nevertheless, he cannot have taken it as too much of an insult, as he continued to exhibit at the Academy until he was almost 80.

At around the same time O'Neill was involved with the Royal Irish Art Union, a body which was an offshoot of an English organisation with a similar name but omitting the word 'Irish'. In 1842 the Union awarded O'Neill a prize of ten pounds for his lithograph of *Gandsey, the Killarney minstrel*[12] (Fig. 4). Two years later, however, he was writing indignant letters, apparently to the *Dublin Evening Packet*, complaining about the Union's policy of buying paintings by English artists. Under the rubric *Ireland*, a note appeared on page 18 of *The Art Union, Monthly Journal of the Fine Arts* for 1 January 1845, criticising an unworthy attack— O'Neill's—in the *Evening Packet* because the Society [the Union] had purchased several pictures painted by English artists. It ran as follows:

> Away with this continual and most pernicious effort to draw a distinction between men born in Ireland and men born in England. The president of the Royal Academy and 7 other members are Irish. We trust the Committee of the Royal Irish Art Union are far too wise and enlightened to listen to so degrading a proposal as we find in *The Evening Packet*—to do so would surely doom the Arts in Ireland to perpetual mediocrity.

Another letter from O'Neill in the *Evening Packet* (recommended by the Editor, no less) was equally condemned by the Art Union journal on page 50 of its issue of February 1845, where it was, however, gracious enough to describe Henry O'Neil (wrongly spelled with only one 'l') as 'a landscape painter, one of the few really good Irish artists who is not an "absentee" '.

On page 16 of the January 1846 issue of *The Art Union* a premium was announced for a lithograph drawn by Mr O'Neill, but on page 154 of the June issue the print intended for issue to subscribers was, according to Strickland, changed from a drawing submitted by O'Neill to one by W. Brocas, entitled *Sunday Morning*, which 'exhibits the interior of an Irish cabin, with peasant girls preparing their "toilet" '.

On page 212 of the same volume, Henry O'Neill's

HENRY O'NEILL OF THE 'CELTIC CROSS'

Fig. 4—*Gandsey, the Killarney minstrel*, an engraving of 1843 in the National Library of Ireland (PD GAND–JA). Courtesy of the National Library of Ireland.

Pl. 4—O'Neill's view c
Castle Howard, Co. W
published by W.F. Wake
in Vol. I of *Picturesque s*
of some of the finest lands
and coast scenery of Irelar
(Dublin, 1835). The ca
says that the castle 'leac
mind to blend togethe
ideas of the age of chiv
with those of the high
polished refinement of
present day'!

picture entitled *Rich and rare were the gems she wore* (doubtless inspired by Thomas Moore's poem of the same name), exhibited as No. 12 in the Exhibition of the Society of Artists, was sarcastically reviewed as showing

> that this artist's forte does not lie in historical or figure subjects, nor can we say much for his landscapes in oils, with the exception of a small one entitled 'A Summer Morning scene, near Bray, County of Wicklow', No. 15, which shows some promise. His watercolour sketches are clever: the best is a trifling one, No. 112, 'View near Dundrum', while several others are 'old stagers,' which we thought would have been inadmissible twice in the same exhibition.

Bad blood there somewhere. But his reputation was rescued somewhat by a long speech given by O'Neill—'an excellent landscape painter'—as reported on page 370 of the December 1845 issue of the journal, in which he argued for the importance of getting an excellent steel-plate engraver from London to produce Fine Art prints in Ireland. This would require assistants and apprentices and, he thought, would help to create a highly lucrative branch of the Fine Arts in Ireland, besides preventing the necessity of importing prints from England and sending works to be engraved in England. Thus, he argued, a profitable export trade would be created while, at the same time, 'taking the best means for improving the taste of the people, as well as increasing the wealth of the country'. Who knows whether he saw himself as a partial beneficiary in such a suggested scheme?

NOTES

1. Peter Murray, *George Petrie (1790–1866): the rediscovery of Ireland's past* (Cork and Kinsale, 2004).

2. Petra Coffey, 'George Victor Du Noyer, 1817–1869: artist, geologist and antiquary', *Journal of the Royal Society of Antiquaries of Ireland* **123** (1993), 102–19.

3. Fionnuala Croke, *George Du Noyer, 1817–1869: hidden landscapes* [exhibition catalogue] (Dublin, 1995). For Wakeman, see P. Harbison, 'Wakeman's *Archaeologia Hibernica*', *Irish Arts Review* **30** (2) (June–August 2013), 118–21.

4. Owen Dudley Edwards, 'Oscar Wilde and Henry O'Neill', *The Irish Book* **1** (1959–62), 12, quoting Gavan Duffy.

5. *The Irish Builder*, 1 April 1880.

6. Walter G. Strickland, *A dictionary of Irish artists*, Vol. II (Dublin/London 1913), 197.

7. Eamonn de Búrca Catalogue No. 100, item no. 402.

8. Gitta Willemson, *The Dublin Society Drawing Schools: students and award winners* (Dublin, 2000), 76.

9. John Turpin, *A School of Art in Dublin since the eighteenth century: a history of the National College of Art and Design* (Dublin, 1995), 110.

10. Rosalind M. Elmes, *National Library of Ireland. Catalogue of Irish topographical prints and original drawings* (ed. Michael Hewson) (Dublin, 1975), 159, no. 2082.

11. *Ibid.*, 158, no. 2077.

12. Now National Library PD GAND-JA (1) 111.

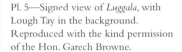

2

LANDSCAPES

As an artist, O'Neill is noteworthy for having worked not only in a variety of media but also in a multiplicity of genres— landscapes, portraiture and antiquarian subjects. From his formative years we know little or nothing of his output, and it is not until he was in his mid-30s that we find him starting to make his mark.

In 1835 he began his publishing career by producing thirteen out of fourteen of the coloured aquatints in a book entitled *Fourteen views in the County of Wicklow* (see p. 3), which he co-authored with Andrew Nicholl, who was the artist of the only other illustration. He used this material in another volume the same year, *Picturesque sketches of some of the finest landscape and coast scenery of Ireland*, in which O'Neill was the last-named of the three authors, the other two being George Petrie and Andrew Nicholl. The book was published by W.F. Wakeman, the father of the well-known antiquarian artist of the same name and initials. Water featured prominently in the subjects covered, which ranged from the *Dargle Valley* and the *Vale of Ovoca* (Avoca) to the *Meeting of the Waters* and *Shelton Abbey* (Pls 1–3). His eye also focused on modern buildings in their landscape settings in the form of *Castle Howard* and *Shelton Abbey* (Pls 3 and 4).

One obvious absentee among the subjects included was Wicklow's most famous attraction, Glendalough, which had become a very popular location for artistic activity from the 1770s onwards. The lacuna may possibly be explained by the appearance of a view of Glendalough as the frontispiece to Major Cosby's book *Kevin's Bed*, produced by a different Dublin publisher, Hardy, in 1835, exactly the same year as the *Fourteen views*. The style of this picture fits in well with O'Neill's penchant for viewing a valley from a distant height (of which more anon) and with the typeface used for the caption, which, although it says that the view was 'taken by the author', may well at least have been a product of O'Neill's paintbox, if not actually of his pen. The colours in the *Fourteen views* are very strong and almost unnatural.

O'Neill's love of framing either side of his pictures with single or multiple trees, which is evidenced in his *Dargle*, *Avoca* and *Meeting of the Waters* pictures in *Fourteen views*, is also evident in a separate watercolour of an unnamed landscape, signed and dated 1835, which was offered by the Cynthia O'Connor Gallery in its exhibition of March–April 1985. On the right-hand side we have a small lake reflecting a building (a chapel?) in the distance, and with a horse-drawn cart and animals not far from the banks. Five years earlier, the same gallery exhibited a very dramatic illustration of *Dunmore Cave* in County Kilkenny (Fig. 5), looking upwards from the weakly lit depths towards the light of the rounded entrance above, with two small figures trying to keep their balance as they tread warily downwards, while at the same time providing a human scale. The picture may date from the time O'Neill spent in Kilkenny around the early 1850s, but, sadly, it has not been possible to trace the present whereabouts of either of these two Cynthia O'Connor Gallery pictures.

The year 1835 was an important one in O'Neill's life, because it was then that he not only began his publishing career but also first exhibited at the Royal Hibernian Academy, a habit which he fortunately continued until one year before his death in 1880. Of his eight pictures on show that year three-quarters were of Wicklow subjects. Though the titles differed from those used in the *Fourteen views*, one was of *Glendalough*, perhaps related to the frontispiece of Cosby's 1835 *Kevin's Bed* book referred to above. Here was featured Glendalough's famous round tower, a genre that was to occupy

Pl. 6—*Banquet in honour of John Crichton in front of Crom Castle, Co. Fermanagh*, after a photograph reproduced by kind permission of the earl of Erne.

Pl. 7—Oil painting probably titled *Mountain cliff over the north side of Dundalk* in the Henry McDowell collection.

Pl. 8 (opposite)—
Watercolour *View of
the City of Dublin
from above Tallaght* in
the Henry
McDowell
collection.

Pl. 9—Oil painting
of *Sunset at
Monasterboice, Co.
Louth*, with round
tower, high crosses
and mourners at a
grave, in the Henry
McDowell
collection.

Pl. 10 (opposite)—
Watercolour of
*Kildare Round Tower
and Cathedral*,
before its
restoration between
1872 and 1896, in
the Henry
McDowell
collection.

Pl. 11—*The Rock of
Cashel, Co.
Tipperary*, in an
unfinished haze in
the background,
from the Henry
McDowell
collection.

Cashel
Co. Tipperary

HENRY O'NEILL OF THE 'CELTIC CROSS'

Pl. 12—Oil painting of *Benburb on the Ulster Blackwater*, site of Owen Roe O'Neill's victorious battle in 1646, from the Dolores Treacy collection.

Pl. 13 (opposite)—*Seated man in a wood*. National Gallery of Ireland (No. 313). Reproduced by kind permission of the National Gallery.

Fig. 5—*Dunmore Cave, Co. Kilkenny.*
Present whereabouts unknown.
Photograph courtesy of TRIARC.

O'Neill's attention in his latter years. Another example, at *Clondalkin* in County Dublin, which probably formed the centre-piece of another of his Academy pictures, was one which he also included as a contribution to the illustrations of Mr and Mrs S.C. Hall's *Ireland: its scenery and character* in 1841–3, for which he also provided north Dublin vignettes of the *High Cross at Finglas* (Fig. 6) and another at the entrance to *St Doulough's church* at Balgriffin (Fig. 7).

O'Neill's mastery of watercolour technique by the second half of the 1830s is demonstrated *inter alia* in two remarkable examples in separate collections which have been preserved for us. The first of these, dated 1836, is a beautiful view of *Luggala* in the Wicklow Hills (Pl. 5), offered by the Gorry Gallery in its exhibition of 22 April–5 May 1988 and which is now preserved by the present owner of Luggala, the Hon. Garech Browne, with whose kind permission it is reproduced here. As was the case with the Glendalough picture mentioned above, here the artist is also on a height, looking down at the romantic corrie lake, Lough Tay, and just visible are the tall chimneys of the house built probably in the early nineteenth century. In the foreground is the typical tree on the left, but the centre foreground is taken up with a charming vignette of two behatted gentlemen chatting over a fallen tree, as a well-dressed woman approaches from the left. Another lady stands motionless in the shadows behind her. Above the two gentlemen, a further figure observes the view from the top of a mound. The contrasting colours of the figures' clothes and the shades of green in the landscape make this one of O'Neill's most satisfying watercolours.

Three years later we find O'Neill up in County Fermanagh creating a remarkable record of a *Presentation banquet for John Crichton*, reproduced here from a photograph by kind permission of the earl of Erne (Pl. 6). On the left are two of the artist's customary trees, while the right-hand side is dominated by the façade and towered *porte-cochère* of the neo-Gothic Crom Castle beside Lough Erne (with its medieval predecessor beside the lake in the background). Between tree and tower are serried rows of banqueters, seated at a dozen parallel tables each accommodating about 50 people, and with a great variety of well-dressed bystanders looking on. It is extraordinary with what precision O'Neill has managed to

delineate so many figures so realistically yet at such a miniature scale, the whole comprising a unique scene of overpowering splendour at the start of the Victorian era.

Had John Ruskin seen it (which he may possibly have done) he would certainly have approved of the Crom Castle picture because he was a great supporter of neo-Gothic, and it is conceivable (though perhaps not very likely) that it was some drawings of the Irish Henry O'Neill and not his English namesake that Ruskin is said to have acquired and given to the university of Oxford, where they cannot be traced. Ruskin was also a great admirer of the paintings of that greatest of English painters J.M.W. Turner, and it is interesting to note the influence of Turner on the largest and finest private collection of O'Neill paintings and watercolours, that of Henry McDowell, to whom this book is dedicated.

The first of these, in oils, is a very dramatic view that was probably entitled *Mountain cliff over the north side of Dundalk* (Pl. 7), taken probably from somewhere near Faughart and, as so often with O'Neill's landscapes, looking down from a height towards the flat land below. What makes the picture so Turneresquely dramatic is the accumulation of dark and threatening clouds which dominate the large expanse of sky, while the rock massif on the left beside the path leading downwards could almost be envisaged as a theatrical backdrop to the Blasted Heath in *Macbeth*—with not a tree in sight, unusually for the artist. The more sombre colouring tones and the location in County Louth could suggest a date no earlier than the 1860s, when the artist had taken up permanent residence in County Louth, but it may well be earlier, as we know that he was up in County Louth by around 1856, when he would have been drawing Monasterboice for his *Sculptured crosses*, published in 1857.

A rather similar composition is to be found in his wonderfully romantic view over *Dublin City*, probably taken from somewhere above Tallaght (Pl. 8) and most likely dating from the later 1830s, around the time of that equally satisfying and charming view of *Luggala*, painted when O'Neill was already at the height of his powers as a watercolourist. In comparison to the *Luggala* picture, the colours are much brighter and friendlier, the sky with gentle cloud covering a lighter shade of blue than that outlining the trees acting as a girdle around the city already beginning to sprawl westwards. The ubiquitous trees of the foreground are verdant with fresh and beautifully painted foliage, while the vegetation in front of them is vernally fluffy. Here, nature's glorious display dwarfs two human figures, which play a subordinate role and which the eye takes time to locate. In a totally different way, the calmness of the scene is reflected in a lifelike study in the same collection of *two sheep* relaxing together on a grassy slope (Pl. 21), demonstrating O'Neill's ability to combine the effects of light and shade.

A further Turneresque feature in another oil painting in the McDowell collection is found in the glowing golden sky emanating from the sun seen setting behind the round tower at *Monasterboice*, Co. Louth (Pl. 9). Here, what was arguably once the tallest round tower in the country (now without its top) dwarfs not only the two ivied medieval chapels but also, more particularly, the three high crosses located at right, left and in the centre, which one would have thought he would have been at pains to bring out more markedly, particularly as the picture was painted around the time when he was preparing his *magnum opus* on high crosses in 1857, in which a similar version appears. The two figures crying over the tombstone of a loved one in the right foreground are slightly reminiscent of the pilgrims in Petrie's decades-earlier views of Clonmacnois, though O'Neill would not have approved of the comparison with his arch-enemy.

It may be noted in passing that a watercolour sold in the Ivey-Selkirk Gallery in St Louis, Missouri, in March 2007 (unlocated) was titled 'Monasterboice' but was in reality the *Gate-house at Mellifont* in the same county, for which no satisfactory illustration was available for reproduction here.

A round tower also features in each of two other remarkable O'Neills in the McDowell collection. One is at Kildare (Pl. 10), showing the round tower with its presumably later crenellations on top, and with a human figure in miniature on the left beside the tower standing mutely in the background. To the right is St Brigid's Cathedral in its ruined state before George Edmund Street restored it between 1872 and 1896, thus providing us with a date *ante quem* for the picture. This is perhaps the only instance where O'Neill devoted the whole centre-piece of a picture to a Gothic church, as castles were his preferred subjects. Another cathedral, accompanied by a scarcely visible round tower, appears in yet another O'Neill picture in the McDowell collection, this time at *Cashel* (Pl. 11) in County Tipperary (which is also the subject of a drawing in the Ulster Museum in Belfast). But here the cathedral and tower are only pencilled in, suggesting that the upper part of the picture was never finished, giving it a somewhat shadowy and fairy-like appearance. The lower half is characterised by a path meandering down from the centre foreground towards the cluster of houses near the foot of St Patrick's Rock. Visible at a small scale on the path are a mother and child, presumably having just left the poor thatched cottage, with a lonesome cow near the centre foreground. The contrast of darker rocky slopes on the left with the sun shining on the bright green field below the trees on the right makes this an attractive, if only half-finished, picture.

One further landscape is worthy of note here, its medium one of the comparatively rare instances where O'Neill used oil on canvas for his landscapes. Signed and dated 1870, it was offered for sale in Adam's in Dublin as lot 0079 on 28 September 2011, with the title given as 'Bendurg'. Its correct title ought to have been *Benburb* (Pl. 12), where Owen Roe O'Neill won a famous victory in 1646. It was presumably this triumph that attracted O'Neill to come and paint the scene where his patriotism and his family pride could combine in full painterly expression, and it is also one of the few instances where we can record O'Neill's presence in what is now Northern Ireland. Benburb Castle is seen on a rock outcrop projecting out from the left at the centre of the picture, overlooking the valley of the (Ulster) River Blackwater, down to which, in true O'Neill style, a dipping field leads in the centre foreground, where a mother and child admire the view. I am grateful to Mrs Dolores Treacy, the current owner of the picture, for her permission to reproduce it here, and to Messrs Adam's for the colour reproduction.

Finally, one picture is totally out of character with the rest of O'Neill's landscapes. This is of a *Seated man in a wood* (Pl. 13), where one has to peep hard to see the man seated beneath a heavy foliage of almost threatening trees, which might be a good subject for study by a psychologist!

It was mentioned above that O'Neill frequently

exhibited at the Royal Hibernian Academy throughout his career, and some of the oils and watercolours just discussed can be identified with probability in its catalogues, summarised so usefully in the valuable volumes by Ann M. Stewart (see Appendix). These include *Luggala* and *Dublin* from the mountainside (probably that described above as the view of Dublin from above Tallaght), exhibited in 1836, as well as 'Hugh O'Neill's Castle—Co. Tyrone', which may be the *Benburb* picture, a 'Mountain Cliff on the North side of Dundalk' (probably the picture of 1871 given that title above), while the pair of *sheep* are probably those exhibited in the following year.

This, however, is less than one-twelfth of all the pictures shown at the Hibernian Academy, and even if we add the portraits and castle pictures discussed in other chapters as having been seen in public—which amounts only to an additional four—we come to the sad conclusion that six-sevenths of O'Neill's pictures listed by Stewart are unaccounted for. Where some of them hopefully still lurk is unknown. When we tot up all of O'Neill's works shown in the Academy, and other finished works not exhibited there but mentioned in various places throughout the text of this volume, we come to well-nigh 100 examples (over and above those sketches in his surviving notebooks) completed over a period of 40 years, and we may well ask where all of those unaccounted-for pictures have gone. Did some of them cross the Atlantic, like the Mellifont picture sold in St Louis, Missouri? Some may actually survive but be kept by their owners rather than going through the sales rooms, and one can only express the hope that this book may bring some more examples to light—although too late for inclusion here!

There are some examples of O'Neill landscapes that include castles, and these are illustrated in subsequent chapters on the subject, but the Hibernian Academy catalogues provide the titles of other castle pictures (listed in the Appendix, pp 101–5), which we do not know to have survived.

Pl. 14—Oil portrait of *John Cornelius O'Callaghan*, author of *A history of the Irish brigades in the service of France.* Now in the National Gallery of Ireland (No. 2222) and reproduced with its permission.

3

PORTRAITS

Many artists could not resist the temptation to create a self-portrait, and Henry O'Neill was no exception. The likeness he drew of himself is now preserved in the National Gallery of Ireland (Frontispiece), one of the few examples of his work that the Gallery possesses. It is on a large sheet, which could be an expression of his own high opinion of his talents. It is a sympathetic pencil portrait of a man probably in his 60s, balding and bearded, his spectacles fronting a benign face with a slight touch of resignation in the eyes at the hard life he had experienced in the interest of his art.

In his *Appeal for pecuniary aid* of 1877 (p. 90), O'Neill stated that, in order to publish his *Sculptured crosses of Ireland* in 1857, he had had to abandon his profession as a portrait painter—a branch of art 'which was very remunerative' and at which he saved money. He first started to exhibit portraits at the Royal Hibernian Academy in 1836, the year after he had first shown his landscapes at the same venue. This was a watercolour of John Barton, Esq., who may possibly have lived in County Wicklow, where O'Neill had worked the previous year. In 1837 he is listed in the Academy catalogue, summarised by Ann M. Stewart, as showing what may have been two separate portraits of Dr R. Graves, probably a relative of the James Graves whom we will see befriending O'Neill in Kilkenny in the 1850s (p. 50).

The following year, the Academy catalogue shows him offering portraits of an unnamed student, as well as an equally anonymous gentleman and his grandmother. For the first time he ventured into the realms of portraying those who strutted the theatrical boards, starting with *Mademoiselle Shieroni* as Amina in Bellini's opera *La Sonnambula*. In 1840 she was followed by *Mr Dawson* as O'Rourke, Prince of Breffni, in the new historical tragedy called *Dermot McMurrough or the Invasion* by the author of *Jephtha's Vow*. What may possibly have been a follow-up to this picture (rather than the picture itself) was *The return of O'Rourke* which, according to Strickland,[1] was selected for engraving by the National Union in 1846 but was later replaced with *Sunday morning* by Brocas. This must have disappointed—not to say disgusted—O'Neill, who nevertheless at least had the satisfaction of having his picture bought by his political hero, Daniel O'Connell. Its whereabouts, and those of other portraits of *A young lady in fancy costume* and of an unnamed gentleman of 1840, together with those of the 1830s mentioned above, sadly remain unknown.

The earliest of his portraits known to survive is that of *Gandsey, the Killarney minstrel* (Fig. 4; see also p. 5), which he probably sketched in 1842 and which we know only from an engraving produced the following year. It shows us the well-dressed (blind?) musician sitting on a suitable stone, playing his uileann pipes, with a large tree and the lakes of Killarney in the background. For the (now lost) original he was, again according to Strickland, awarded a prize of ten pounds by the Royal Irish Art Union in 1842.

One of his rare pencil portraits to survive is the engaging, if slightly dark, rendition of another blind artistic performer, Michael Moran, better known as Zozimus (*c.* 1794–1846), a famous Dublin balladeer and author of 'The finding of Moses in the bulrushes', the start of which runs as follows:

On Egypt's banks contaygious to the Nile,
The old Pharaoh's daughter went to bathe in style.
She took her dip and came unto the land,
And for to dry her royal pelt she ran along the strand.
A bulrush tripped her, whereupon she saw
A smiling babby in a wad of straw.
She took him up and said in accents mild,
Tear an ages, girls, which of yez owns the child?

Fig. 8—*Michael Moran, better known as Zozimus, the balladeer*. Original drawing in the Joly Collection of the National Library of Ireland (PD EP MORA-MI).

Fig. 9—Undated lithograph of Daniel O'Connell, reproduced by kind permission of the Royal Irish Academy.

I am
yours affectionately,
J. G. Morrison

Lacking any of Gandsey's trimmings, Zozimus (Fig. 8) is shown as a likeable, if slightly sad, man, unperturbed by his lack of sight and keeping himself warm with a long cloak, perhaps waiting for an opportunity to start reciting one of his ballads, which he also distributed in printed sheets around the streets of Dublin. The drawing is now part of the Joly collection in the National Library of Ireland.

O'Neill's lithographic portrait of Daniel O'Connell (Fig. 9), in an engraving probably of the 1830s and now preserved in the Royal Irish Academy in Dublin (RRG/27/11), shows the vibrant Liberator looking almost like an American film star, with assiduously groomed hair and the eyes and smile of a successful lawyer, holding a scroll in his hand. This portrait is one of O'Neill's most engaging, which is not surprising, as he was such a fan of the sitter. O'Neill also did another of O'Connell as lord mayor of Dublin around 1841. His only known watercolour portrait is of a charming, ringletted lady (Fig. 12).

Most of O'Neill's portraits are known only from lithographed versions after his own (lost) originals. One of the earliest of these is a mezzotint (Fig. 10) of Bartholomew Lloyd (1772–1837), seated with the dignity one would expect of a provost of Trinity College, Dublin, and president of the Royal Irish Academy, but this was not issued until a year after the subject's death. With the exception of O'Connell, O'Neill rarely portrayed his sitter as smiling, and nowhere is this more evident than in his portrait of the surgeon John William Cusack (1853), who has the look of a serious medical professional without any obvious sense of humour, and seeming to sport a somewhat red nose. Earnestness is the hallmark of the (undated) Protestant divine S.G. Morrison (Fig. 11), who holds a book (the Bible?) in his left hand and gestures with his right in an effort to convince an audience of his religious zeal.

Another who holds a book, but keeping it open with his finger at the page where he was reading before being interrupted to have his likeness taken, is John 'Secundus' Purser (Fig. 13), described by his descendant Michael Purser[2] as 'tough, shrewd and uncompromising', with a figure 'becoming to a brewer'— and a very successful one at that, as he was an important partner of Sir Benjamin Lee Guinness in expanding the Guinness brewery in the first half of the nineteenth century. John 'Secundus' lived from 1783 to 1858, and his portrait was completed probably towards the end of his life, or at least years after he had already been painted by his cousin Frederick William Burton.[3]

It may be noted that, in addition to making lithographs of his own originals, O'Neill also did at least five others, after daguerreotypes by Professor Gluckman, copies of which are now preserved in the National Gallery. A number of the men represented were involved in politics, some of them inmates with O'Connell in the Richmond Bridewell (see p. 36). They include Sir Edward Blakeney (1778–1868), Terence Bellew MacManus (c. 1823–61), Thomas Francis Meagher (1823–67), William Smith O'Brien (1803–64) and Richard O'Gorman (1820–95).

It would seem that, when O'Neill did return to portraiture, he painted at least one in oils, that of John Cornelius O'Callaghan (Pl. 14), author of a *History of the Irish brigade in the service of France* and a man whose political views rather resembled O'Neill's. Dressed in black on a sombre background, the picture focuses on the bright skin tones of the face and bald head and was probably a realistic likeness. Numbered 313 in the National Gallery's collection, it is undated but probably from around the same time as the portraits of the Revd Thaddeus O'Malley, author of *Home Rule on the basis of federalism*, and Professor Glover, of 1874–5. After the artist's death, it was probably his widow Juliet who exhibited a portrait of herself in the Irish Exhibition of Arts and Manufactures in 1882, and another of the Revd J. O'Hanlon, presumably he of the multi-volume *Lives of the Irish saints*. It should be noted that the portrait of (presumably the Admiral) Horatio Nelson listed by Ann Stewart is more likely to be by the artist's English counterpart, Henry Nelson O'Neil. For the portrait of Oscar Wilde attributed to O'Neill see Chapter 12 (p. 89).

NOTES

1. W.G. Strickland, *A dictionary of Irish artists*, Vol. 2 (Dublin, 1913).
2. Michael Purser, *Jellett, O'Brien, Purser and Stokes. Seven generations, four families* (Dublin, 2004), 34.
3. *Ibid.*, 56.

Fig.13—Lithograph of John 'Secundus' Purser, reproduced by kind permission of the National Library of Ireland (PD EP PURS–JO).

4

O'NEILL, O'CONNELL AND
THE YOUNG IRELANDERS

Pl. 15(a)—The governor's garden in the
Richmond Bridewell, 1844. Reproduced
by kind permission of the National
Museum of Ireland.

Towards the end of the introductory chapter we saw O'Neill's nationalism emerging in public in 1845, railing against the National Art Union's purchase of paintings by English artists. But his political tendencies were already being expressed in art, as witnessed by his watercolours and lithographs from the previous year. It was then that the Liberator, Daniel O'Connell, and a small band of his followers were convicted of conspiring against the state and subsequently imprisoned in the Richmond Bridewell, on the site of the present Griffith College on Dublin's South Circular Road. Their quarters could best be described, however, not as penal but as palatial, for these convicted felons were treated like royalty in captivity. This we know because one of their number, Thomas M. Ray, commissioned O'Neill to do a series of watercolours, nineteen in all, illustrating various aspects of life in the Bridewell (Pls 15 a–d).

The two main concentrations of subject-matter were the bedrooms and sitting-rooms of the various inmates. It was as if an interior decorator were brought in to design special beds and to ensure that more than adequate examples of the best and most up-to-date furniture were provided for the comfort of the prisoners. Carpets, tables, chairs, armchairs, writing bureaux, bookshelves, washstands, pictures on the wall (including a map of Ireland hanging sideways) and drapes on the windows all add to the seemingly opulent surroundings, which must have made it difficult to leave after four months of incarceration. Though not the best of the pictures, one shows O'Connell, wearing his 'Milesian hat' (see below), presiding at the top of a table in a large hall, surrounded by his fellow prisoners and their guests, male and female, all dressed formally for the occasion

(Pl. 15(d)). Another depicts the prisoners (again with ladies present) kneeling down in pews in front of the well-appointed altar of the private chapel within the walls. For recreation, the gardens of the governor (Mr Purdon) and the deputy governor (Mr Cooper) stood at the group's disposal, and these O'Neill depicts in their floral summer raiment (Pl. 15(a)). One of the watercolours provides a somewhat austere view of the gaol yard with the high walls of a penitentiary, but another has as its central feature a mound, on top of which stands a lookout turret and which O'Connell *et al.* called 'Tara Hill', the site of O'Connell's last great triumph, which had taken place on this residence of the ancient Irish kings the previous year.

These watercolours are preserved in the Collins Barracks section of the National Museum in Dublin, where they were kindly shown to me by Sandra Heise, having been bought at the Dublin auction house of James Adam's and Sons in 1990/1. But another state institution, the National Gallery, has a fascinating collection of daguerreotypes, not of the bed- and sitting-rooms but of the prisoners themselves, which must have been taken in the prison, as their personnel corresponds exactly to that of the inmates. Underneath each of the daguerreotypes is a signature of the person represented, and these signatures correspond exactly to those on a decorative sheet presented to Edmund William O'Mahony, which was written in the Bridewell in 1844 and is now preserved in the new museum in Glasnevin cemetery, close to where Daniel O'Connell's body lies in the crypt of the round tower.

The daguerreotypes are among the earliest known and dated examples of what was a new photographic technique, invented in Paris only five years earlier. To see the faces of

Pl. 15(b) (next page)—Charles Gavan Duffy's bedroom in the Richmond Bridewell, 1844. Reproduced by kind permission of the National Museum of Ireland.

the individuals, one has to turn the images around and about to get the right angle, but O'Connell can be seen to wear a highly unusual tall hat, presumably the Milesian or 'Repeal' Cap, modelled on an imaginary ancient Irish crown, which the painter Henry MacManus and the sculptor John Hogan had presented to O'Connell at a Monster Meeting in Mullaghmast, Co. Kildare, in 1843. In addition to O'Connell, the other figures present in the National Gallery's collection, to which Anne Hodge kindly drew my attention, were Thomas Steele (described in the Glasnevin paper as 'the Pacificator'), the Liberator's son John, Thos Matthew Ray (who commissioned the watercolours), Charles Gavan Duffy and Richard Barrett. The only daguerreotype missing (whereabouts unknown; lost?) is that of John Gray, later editor of the *Freeman's Journal*, who has one statue erected to him in Glasnevin Cemetery and another on Dublin's O'Connell Street, facing south towards his hero, Daniel O'Connell.

O'Neill had a further engagement with most of these individuals, having made lithographs of some of them, after daguerreotypes made by Leon Gluckman of Abbey Street in Dublin, a Turk, according to David Davison (who got his information from Eddie Chandler). These included Charles Gavan Duffy[1] and Richard O'Gorman Junior.[2] If O'Neill did lithographs of the other Richmond Bridewell inmates, they are not present in the National Gallery's collection. It does, however, have copies of O'Neill lithographs of other Young Irelanders, William Smith O'Brien (in Kilmainham Gaol)[3] and the nationalists John Martin,[4] Terence Bellew McManus (in the dock at Clonmel Courthouse, 11 October 1848)[5] and Thomas Francis Meagher.[6] One of the Smith O'Brien lithographs was acquired from J.V. McAlpine, while others were presented by various members

of the individual's families. These lithographs were issued by Gluckman in 1848, four years after O'Connell and his followers had been incarcerated in their 'five-star' surroundings in the Richmond Bridewell, and it is interesting to note that the various lithographs of Terence Bellew McManus were dedicated by him to various recipients from the same Richmond Gaol in the months of November and December 1848, one of them reproduced in a *Supplement to the Irish Fireside* of 16 September 1885.[7] Independently of all of these, O'Neill also did an undated lithograph of Daniel O'Connell[8] which was printed by R. Martin in London (Fig. 9). Finally, other O'Neill lithographic portraits after daguerreotypes include Lieut.-General Sir Edward Blakeney,[9] also published in 1848 by Gluckman, who dedicated it to the countess of Clarendon, and George Baldwin, registrar of the Court of Exchequer and secretary of St Patrick's Masonic Lodge, published in Dublin by T. Cranfield (undated).[10]

NOTES

1. Adrian Le Harivel (ed.), *National Gallery of Ireland, illustrated summary catalogue of prints and sculpture* (Dublin, 1988), 179, no. 10,179; 180, no. 10,525; and 181, no. 11,935.

2. *Ibid.*, 179, no. 10,522; 181, no. 11,937.

3. *Ibid.*, 178, no. 10,064, and 179, no. 10,521.

4. *Ibid.*, 178, no. 10,102, and 180, no. 11,934.

5. *Ibid.*, 178–9, no. 10,121; 180, no. 10,533; and 182, no. 11,940.

6. *Ibid.*, 179–80, no. 10,523; 181–2, no. 11,938; and 182, no. 10,306.

7. *Ibid.*, 177, no. 20,217.

8. *Ibid.*, 387, no. 10,980.

9. *Ibid.*, 181, no. 10,722.

10. *Ibid.*, 180, no. 10,710.

Pl. 15(c) (previous page)—Daniel O'Connell's bedroom in the Richmond Bridewell, 1844. Reproduced by kind permission of the National Museum of Ireland.

Pl. 15(d) (opposite)—Daniel O'Conn (second from right) wearing his Miles or 'Repeal' Cap, presiding at a dinner his friends in the Richmond Bridewe 1844. Reproduced by kind permissio the National Museum of Ireland.

5

IRISH CASTLES—I:
MUNSTER AND SOUTH LEINSTER

In his book *Ireland for the Irish* of 1868 (see p. 69), O'Neill says that he spent fourteen years of his life in England.[1] Some he spent in the mid-1850s working on his *Sculptured high crosses*, others remain unaccounted for, but, according to Strickland,[2] he went to London in 1847. There he was unable to find work and, after suffering much privation, enlisted in the army, for which he was probably totally unsuited, and had to be bought out by his friends. By 1850 he must have returned to Ireland, for we find him active in Munster in January 1851, drawing castles in particular, and reverting thereby to something he had started at least a decade before, as page 50 of his Sketch-book G provides us with two sketches of Tymon Castle (Fig. 14) near Tallaght (demolished almost exactly 50 years ago), which, O'Neill says, he sketched in 1840. The lost sketch-books would probably have added many more to his list of what he was doing at the time, but his Sketch-book B provides us at least with details of his mid-life industry in recording these tower-houses of the past. This consists of both pencil sketches—which are probably his original field sketches—and pen and blue ink drawings worked up perhaps decades later.

O'Neill may thus, from the age of 40, have been planning to do a country-wide survey of these monuments, which are fortunately still so common in the Irish countryside. Nevertheless, poring over their traces in the Ordnance Survey six-inch sheets which had only recently been issued, he must have realised that so many of them had survived that it would be impossible to do a survey of them all by himself. James N. Healy's *The castles of County Cork* of 1998 counted well over 400 specimens in that county alone, to visit which occupied him for seven years. In the summer of 1851 O'Neill managed to visit just over a score—or, at least, that is what we know of from his surviving sketch-books preserved in Glenstal Abbey. His choice of Cork castles may well have been dictated through advice proffered by his friend John Windele, the Cork antiquary, who knew the castles of his native county intimately—as we know from his album of castle watercolours of around the 1830s preserved in the Royal Irish Academy,[3] which has never seen the light of day, though it certainly deserves to be published. The absence of important castles such as Blarney and Barryscourt among O'Neill's drawings is obviously best explained by the probability that they would have been present in one or other of the lost notebooks.

During his travels of about three months' duration in that summer of 1851, O'Neill examined castles located in the environs of three urban centres—Clonmel, Fermoy and, to a lesser extent, Midleton. There is no suggestion that he was doing this for a patron, nor do we find any evidence that the fruit of his labours in this branch of antiquity was ever published. It is only in his watercolours exhibited at various venues (as listed in the Appendix) that we find his sketches being offered for sale—and public acclamation.

O'Neill describes each castle he visits in considerable detail, occasionally to the point of tedium, which is not necessary to repeat or even synopsise here because of more modern versions available in Healy's above-mentioned book and in the various volumes of the state's County Archaeological Surveys. To those lengthy descriptions O'Neill has added headings in a different ink, making it much easier to find the relevant passage covering the location, entrance, floor, stairs, hall, inner machicolation, spyhole, 'battlements', shot-holes, fireplaces, garderobes etc., while also giving details of the various floors and rooms contained within the walls of each castle. One unusual item which grabbed his attention was the yett, or iron grille (Fig. 15), and its attached chain, which was used to open or close the door. Perhaps his interest in the subject was whetted by John O'Donovan's translation of a passage from the *Annals of the Four Masters* of 1590,[4] where an iron chain featured in the escape of Hugh O'Neill and Hugh O'Donnell from Dublin Castle—a subject on which Henry O'Neill received information by letter from a Dublin barrister, John P. Prendergast of Merrion Square, who also told him of castles near Nenagh and in County Tyrone. Another historical incident in which such an iron chain featured was that involving John Bale, the Protestant bishop of Ossory, who was attacked in 1664 by a mob who killed ten members of his Kilkenny household but who saved himself by being able to shut the iron grate of his castle of Bishop's Court. To his note, O'Neill later added the remark that 'This bishop, from his irritable temper, has been called "bilious Bale".[5] He wrote mysteries [i.e. mystery plays] which were performed at the Market Cross in Kilkenny.'

What are of greater interest to us than his lengthy descriptions are O'Neill's charming pencil and pen sketches of these Munster castles which he visited in 1851, as preserved in his Sketch-book K. A number of these illustrated here are more correctly termed 'tower-houses' in modern parlance, and they are shown in their landscape background as it existed in the middle of the nineteenth century. Fortunately a number of them are still preserved, but the historical value of his sketches is that—like those of his predecessor Gabriel Beranger almost a century earlier—some of them depict structures which have since fallen victim to decay or demolition or, in the case of Castle Inch, have been submerged in the Electricity Supply Board's flooding of the River Lee in creating the Inniscarra dam.

It must have been fairly cold when O'Neill went out hunting his castles in January 1851. He started in Tipperary before concentrating on Cork. His first stop was on 5 January at *Castle Blake*, some eight miles from Clonmel, beside which his sketch shows a splendid collection of haystacks to provide

Fig. 14—*Tymon (Timmons) Castle*, Co. Dublin (demolished), as sketched by O'Neill in 1840 (Glenstal Sketch-book G, p. 50).

Fig. 16—A coy maiden at the door of a County Cork castle (Glenstal Sketch-book K, p. 9).

cattle with their winter fodder. This is a gabled castle with a single tall chimney but no battlements; the measurements 35ft by 26ft are given in a pen and wash plan. O'Neill also provides us with a cross-section, showing the vault above the second floor, and a small drawing of a window with shot-holes beside it. That there were probably other castles on the Cork Blackwater in the lost notebooks is made likely by the watercolour of *Carrigacunna Castle* near Killavullen which was sold, together with another, in Sotheby's Slane Castle sale of 3 November 1981.

Two days later he went to *Lisronan Castle*, three miles north of Clonmel, where, on a single page numbered 9, we find a neat single drawing of the castle and another of a coy maiden standing in the doorway (Fig. 16), below whose elbow is a worn-away chain-hole—a feature also found at the next castle he visited, at *Rathdrum*, not far away, also on 12 January.

On 19 January, having crossed the county border into Cork, he visited the stump of a castle at what he calls *Ballyhone* (probably *Ballynahown*), north of Fermoy, and continued on the same day to what he calls *Ballyhoulam* (probably *Ballyhindon*), which he admits is 'in ruins, so much that nothing of interest is to be found among them—the situation is eminently picturesque', as he shows in a sketch on page 24.

His next port of call is unusual in being round, one of probably less than a dozen or so late medieval examples of its kind in the country. This was *Carrigabrick*, which he records in one neat pencil sketch with cross-section featuring a double vault. The castle is situated on the edge of a steep precipice above the River Blackwater; a quarter of a century ago Healy noted that 'it is a steep climb to the top where the castle stands, and this is achieved mainly by hanging on to bits of trees', and O'Neill may not have found it easy to reach either. Eight years later, O'Neill painted the castle in oils (Pl. 16), the largest and most expensive (£40!) canvas he ever executed, which is now in the possession of Michael and Marianne Gorman.

The next castle is an example of the historical value of O'Neill's sketches. This is *Garrycloyne*, three miles north of Blarney, the dangerous condition of which forced the

county council to demolish it about half a century ago. Even in his day—16 March 1851—O'Neill described it as being 'in a very ruined state', his attractive pen sketch showing a gap in the wall as if a mouse had been gnawing at it. In April, having inspected *Cloghphillip Castle*, one side of which had fallen, O'Neill went south across the Blackwater to *Ballincollig*, now close to modern housing but still in green countryside a century and a half ago, as seen in two attractive sketches demonstrating the structure's location on a raised hillock, well chosen for defence.

That same month he went upstream across the Lee to *Castle Inch*, impressively sited on a bluff above the river's southern bank, but to find it today it would be necessary to don snorkelling gear, as it has vanished beneath the waters held in check by the Inniscarra dam.

Poor O'Neill must have felt not just the cold but doubtless also the rain in hunting castles during the first four months of 1851 in both Tipperary and Cork, but things must have looked up by the time May came with a whiff of summer in the air. He must have walked up the River Bride until he came to *Kilcrea Castle*, not far from an attractive bridge which he places in the foreground of his pen and wash sketch on page 63 of the Glenstal Sketch-book K (Fig. 2). In his notebook description he devotes ten pages to the castle, but dismisses the important neighbouring 'abbey' as being more extensive than picturesque, revealing that his artistic interest was prevailing over his archaeological curiosity; the only item in the abbey to catch his eye was the joggled mantelpiece, of which he gives a miniature drawing. A week later he had crossed the Lee again, this time heading northwards up the River Dripsey to the castle of that name, otherwise known as *Carrignamuck* (Fig. 17), sited on a very prominent rock above the river, as seen in a beautifully atmospheric pen and wash sketch on page 73, to which O'Neill attached a plan with detailed measurements. On page 78 he also provides us with a pair of pen sketches of the castle and its doorway.

The following week he headed north-westwards from Cork City to the now demolished *Ballyvodane Castle*, ten miles away, together with an earthen ringfort and stone circle nearby, on the top and bottom of page 83. Five days later he had changed direction again, this time heading ten miles eastwards to *Belvelly/Belvally* (Fig. 18) on Great Island near Fota, which has changed little since O'Neill drew it on page 84, with two men in a boat close by. Men afloat also feature in his sketch of *Carrigaline Castle*, which he visited on 25 May before reaching *Aghamarta* on the same day. Not far away is *Ballea*, where O'Neill was too rushed to draw the hinged door-grill with chain attached, although he sketched it from memory decades later. The beginning of June saw him once more on the move, this time to near Inishannon on the Bandon River to visit *Kilbeg*, a castle once inhabited by the daughter of the poet Edmund Spenser, author of *The faerie queene*. As O'Neill's sketch indicates, it was 'nearly gone' in his day, and has now completely disappeared, but his plan of it shows how the walls were protected by a fosse or ditch twenty feet wide and twelve feet deep in places. Close by is *Downdaniel Castle*, well known to those travelling the road between Inishannon and Bandon and, unusually, sited at the confluence of two rivers, in this instance the Brinny and the Bandon. The ivy which still covers it was already smothering the walls in O'Neill's day, yet not so completely as to prevent him from showing on page 118 the essential interior structure of the half of the castle that had not collapsed. The final castle in O'Neill's Glenstal Sketch-book K is *Ballintotis*, located between Midleton and Castlemartyr, the most easterly of the Cork castles that he visited, which involved him doubling back on his journey to Belvelly the previous month.

O'Neill needed just half a year to visit the twenty or so castles in the notebook, and the fact that, in certain cases, his inspections were a week apart might suggest that he was in gainful employment during the working week somewhere in the Cork area, and it may have been only at weekends that he could foray forth to seek out his tower-houses. What surprises, however, is his choice of castles.

By December 1851 O'Neill was back in Dublin, sketching *Dunsoghly Castle* and its doorway and *Puck's Castle* near Ballycorus, which he visited on Christmas Day, suggesting that, at that stage, he had not yet any family to be with at Yuletide. Having sketched this 'small mountain

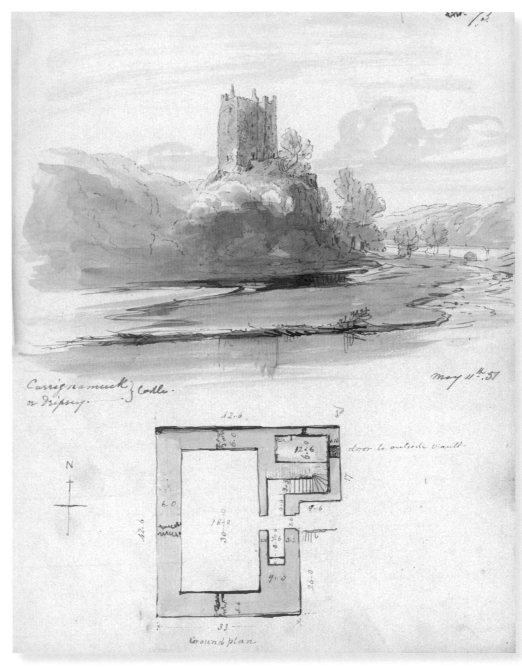

Fig. 17—*Carrignamuck* or *Dripsey Castle*, Co. Cork, sketched by O'Neill in May 1851 (Glenstal Sketch-book K, p. 73).

Fig. 18—*Belvelly Castle*, Co. Cork, as sketched by O'Neill in May 1851 (Glenstal Sketch-book K, p. 84).

Fig. 19—*Clone Castle, Co. Kilkenny* (Glenstal Sketch-book G, p. 102).

Fig. 21—Man seated on *Kilree High
Cross, Co. Kilkenny* (Glenstal Sketch-
book G, p. 93).

Fig. 20—*Castle in Maudlin Street,
Kilkenny*, drawn by O'Neill on 22 August
1872 (Glenstal 'Antiquities' volume,
unnumbered page).

fortress . . . on a wild rocky hill', he visited Mount Venus dolmen, also on the slopes of the Dublin Mountains, a week later on New Year's Eve (see below, p. 65).

By 18 January 1852 O'Neill was down in Kilkenny visiting *Ballynaboley Castle*, then *Cantwell's Castle* and, in the following month, the 'greatly dilapidated' *Drakeland Castle*, once associated with Bishop Berkeley. Subsequent months saw him visiting the castles of *Clone* (Fig. 19) and *Cloghscregg*, and then, for a change, *Fertagh* with its tall round tower, which he noted, and followed, finally, in November 1852 by *Aghaviller Castle*. It was probably at around this time that he sketched an attractive view of a tower-house in Maudlin Street, Kilkenny (Fig. 20). It was also during this period that we first come across O'Neill showing an interest in high cross sites: he noted an inscription on a slab beside the high cross at *Killamery*, Co. Kilkenny, sketched a man sitting on the base of the *Kilree* cross (Fig. 21) and gives a drawing of one of the crosses at what he calls *Kilclispeen*,

better known nowadays as *Ahenny*. This he had traced from an original by Dr James Graves, who was very prominent in the Kilkenny Archaeological Society, which had been founded only three years earlier and which was to be the ancestor of the Royal Society of Antiquaries of Ireland, the country's premier archaeological society.

NOTES

1. Henry O'Neill, *Ireland for the Irish. A practical, peaceable, and just solution of the Irish Land Question* (London/Dundalk, 1868), 53.
2. Walter G. Strickland, *A dictionary of Irish artists* (Dublin/London, 1913), 199.
3. Royal Irish Academy, MS 12 M 15.
4. John O'Donovan (ed.), *Annals of the kingdom of Ireland by the Four Masters, from the earliest period to the year 1616* (Dublin, 1848–51), Vol. 6, 1898–9.
5. O'Neill's Sketch-book K, p. 109.

Pl. 17—Through colouring the various strands of interlace on Monasterboice and other crosses, O'Neill was able to demonstrate for the first time that high crosses must have been coloured. From *The sculptured crosses of ancient Ireland*.

6

THE SCULPTURED CROSSES OF ANCIENT IRELAND

While in Cork in 1851–2, O'Neill cannot but have been aware of the preparations for a great exhibition in the city in 1852, which the country was later able to read about in John Francis Maguire's *Industrial movement in Ireland, as illustrated by the National Exhibition of 1852*, published in Cork the following year. Its very title announced that what had started out as a Cork city and county initiative had grown into one of national significance. In the author's words, the exhibition was 'initiated by the desire to foster local industry after the calamity of the Famine, to inspire confidence in local industrial quality, and to overcome prejudice in favour of English manufacture'. O'Neill's friend John Windele wrote the 'Irish Antiquities' section of the catalogue on pages 349–67, where he starts off by telling a revealing anecdote:

> The late Doctor Brinkley [bishop] of Cloyne was one of that class of thinkers who could only discern, in the long vista of Ireland's past history, some faint shadowings of naked unskilled savages, lurking in the obscurity of primaeval forests, or basking in their lairs, ignorant of every art. In the fullness of his complacent ignorance, he once said to one of our archaeologists, in a learned assembly, 'Surely, sirs, you do not mean to tell us, that there exists the slightest evidence to prove that the Irish had any acquaintance with the arts of civilized life, anterior to the arrival in Ireland of the English'.

With the Cork Exhibition displaying such objects as ogham stones, the Shrine of St Patrick's Bell, the Tara Brooch (deposited by the Dublin jeweller Waterhouse), the Cross of Cong (Fig. 42), lent by the Royal Irish Academy, the Lismore Crozier (Pl. 19), sent for exhibition by the duke of Devonshire, and a copy of 'Brian Boru's Harp', it is no wonder that Windele could then comment that 'such articles afford a ready answer to the flippant caviler, and the self-sufficient opacity of the Utilitarian, who can discover no evidence of either civilization or progress in Ancient Ireland until she had been schooled by her stern Saxon teachers'. It was this kind of rhetoric that was to inflame O'Neill's imagination over the next two decades.

Dublin followed Cork's example the following year by mounting a truly National Exhibition in a glass-covered hall on the lawn outside Leinster House, which, in turn, had also been inspired by the Great Exhibition of 1851 in London's Crystal Palace. James Mahony's watercolour portrayal of the scene (National Gallery) when Queen Victoria and Prince Albert came to admire it shows two high crosses standing proud on the left-hand side, the first time that such venerable Irish monuments were ever intentionally presented to the public, having been brought from their age-old locations at Kells, Co. Meath, and Kilkieran, Co. Kilkenny (another cross from Tuam, Co. Galway, is not visible in the picture). Henry O'Neill may well have played a role in having the Kilkenny cross displayed in Dublin, for at a meeting of the burgeoning Kilkenny and South-East of Ireland Archaeological Society in November 1852 attention was drawn[1] to 'a splendid series of drawings of the ancient sculptured crosses of the county of Kilkenny which ornamented the walls of the meeting room on that day', of which that at Kilkieran was presumably one (Fig. 22a). It transpired that the Revd James Graves had pointed out the location of these crosses to 'the

able artist now sojourning in Kilkenny, Mr. Henry O'Neill; that gentleman, with a genuine antiquarian zeal only equalled by his skill as a draughtsman, had devoted much of his time and labour to the production of the very beautiful and most faithful drawings' before the meeting. Mr Graves then stated that it was Mr O'Neill's intention to illustrate the crosses of County Kilkenny by lithography, in which department he was a practised hand. He proposed to publish, as a commencement, six tinted lithographs, imperial folio, in a suitable folding case, of which a prospectus would immediately be issued. This would seem to be the earliest printed record we have of O'Neill's interest in high crosses, though it is surprising that they never featured in all the works he exhibited at the Royal Hibernian Academy or elsewhere. In a letter to Windele in June 1853[2] O'Neill included a copy of the prospectus or flyer of his planned work, a copy of which is preserved in the Royal Irish Academy.[3] Here the planned title was given simply as *Ancient crosses of Ireland*, and the text ran as follows:

There are a great many ANCIENT STONE CROSSES in Ireland, which, from their size, noble proportions, and richness of decoration, are impressive and beautiful memorials of the refinement and piety of the ancient Irish; they are also peculiarly national, both in form and ornaments. The most interesting of these will be selected; they will be carefully measured, and the ornamental details given with all possible accuracy.

The work will be completed in Six Parts, imperial folio (22 inches by 15), each Part to contain six Lithographic Prints and descriptive Letter-press.

PRICE PER PART

PRINTS WITH TINT STONE ... £1 1 0

COLOURED IN IMITATION OF THE ORIGINAL DRAWINGS ... £2 2 0

An Introductory Essay on Irish Crosses, and a suitable Title-Page will be given with the concluding Part.

H. O'NEILL (of KILKENNY), ARTIST.

Publishers: Messrs. ACKERMAN and Co., 96, Strand; GEORGE BELL, 186, Fleet-street; and E. Gambart and Co., 25 Berners-street, Oxford-street, London.

To which O'Neill added by hand: '& Hodges and Smith, Grafton St., Dublin'.

In the autumn of 1854 O'Neill made a visit to Clonmacnois to make further drawings and rubbings for his proposed book on the ancient crosses of Ireland; in addition to the crosses he made rubbings of the memorial slabs, of which Clonmacnois has the finest collection in these islands. He employed[4] an intelligent 'native' to make rubbings with grass and to produce facsimile after facsimile. O'Neill subsequently went over the rubbing thus made, 'tracing in, with a soft pencil, any line which the roughness of the material—a fissile sand-stone—rendered indistinct on the rubbing'. 'Perfect accuracy had thus been secured', declared a delighted Graves, while also deprecating[5] the daily depredations that had been practised on the stones—portable examples being carried away as souvenirs, or being removed by the peasantry to serve as gravestones elsewhere (*plus ça change!*). Graves was saddened that some of the stones that had been drawn on site by Petrie almost a quarter of a century earlier were not present among O'Neill's collection, as they had probably been removed or stolen in the meantime, and Graves went so far as to level some criticism at Petrie[6] for not having published a number of his drawings. Some of this comment may conceivably have been coming from O'Neill himself, who, over time, was becoming more and more vociferous in his criticism of Petrie, and who would have been pleased to get support for his view from any quarter. Graves submitted the list of O'Neill's rubbings to the great Celtic scholar and friend of Petrie John O'Donovan, who replied[7] that he had seen a number of the Clonmacnois stones in 1838 but that there were some of which he had no recollection whatsoever. 'Mr O'Neill has probably found some which were dug up since I was there', noted O'Donovan. Graves[8] suggested that people would be amply repaid by a visit to Mr O'Neill, who was residing in Kilkenny at the time, when they could examine not only the rubbings of these monumental stones but also Mr O'Neill's ample collection of drawings and rubbings made to illustrate the great work on which he was, with noble enthusiasm, employed. These are probably those preserved in the Bodleian Library in Oxford under the accession number Ir. Top A.3.

According to a letter preserved in the Royal Irish Academy, O'Neill was writing to Windele years later to encourage the creation of a memorial to Graves for all the work he had done—perhaps not surprisingly, as Graves was indeed very supportive of O'Neill. At a meeting of the Kilkenny Society in March 1855,[9] Graves expressed the hope that a fund could be established to engrave those Clonmacnois gravestones—'about £15 would be sufficient'—and feared that 'for want of patronage of the public, Mr O'Neill might not be able to accomplish all he intended'. This appeal was published in a local newspaper but was answered by O'Neill in the form of a letter to the public,[10] saying that he did not need the patronage as he had it from the leading nobility and gentry of Ireland, from the duke of Leinster downward! In addition, he quoted support from the Royal Society of Antiquaries (of London) and the Archaeological Institute of Great Britain and Ireland, and had been mentioned in flattering terms in the catalogues of the Crystal Palace at Sydenham (site of the Great London Exhibition of 1851). In his letter, dated March 1855, O'Neill went on to point out that he had originally intended issuing three dozen prints of the high crosses and had accepted advice that he should provide letterpress at no extra cost to the subscribers and add an essay on early Irish art. To this he adds that

I have all the materials ready[11] for completing the work, which I purpose going on with as soon as I reach London. In a word, I consider that, for one who is a stranger to the public, my success with this, my first

publication, is such as ought to gratify the most sanguine expectations; meantime, I know that my good friend, the Rev. J. Graves, only expressed himself as he did through the most kindly feeling, partly induced thereto from his knowledge of the great labour I have been at in order to make myself master of the greatest development of ornamental art the world has ever produced—the Fine Art of ancient Ireland.

Even though his later instalments of the lithographs of the crosses had yet to appear, in 1855 O'Neill was already declaring himself author of the work on *The ancient crosses of Ireland* in one of his first major public utterances, *A descriptive catalogue of illustrations of the fine arts of ancient Ireland . . . and serving to show, that a truly national and beautiful style of art existed in Ireland from a remote period till some time after the Anglo-Norman invasion*, published by O'Neill himself at his then Dublin address of 23 Aungier Street. The text was an accompaniment to a series of three lectures which O'Neill planned to give—and, indeed, gave in Belfast in November 1855, as reported in the *Belfast Mercury* at the time,[12] as well as near Rostellan in County Cork,[13] though doubtless also in other places of which we have no record. We can see from O'Neill's letters addressed to his antiquarian friend John Windele (preserved in the Royal Irish Academy) that he plagued Windele with requests to set up lectures for him with the Cork Institution, or anyone else who would host him and at least pay his expenses, if not add a little more.

In this *Catalogue of illustrations* for his lectures, O'Neill expounds for the first time in public his great missionary idea that the Irish crosses, intended to be painted in various colours, were superior to anything in England, and that their designers or executors were consummate masters of decorative art. The same, he said, also applied to metalwork. In a fit of national exuberance, he proclaimed that the artists of ancient Ireland excelled those of other nations in ornamental art, and were unequalled in Europe. Most of the ornament applied was very elaborate and intricate as well as beautiful, and so infinitely varied as to never repeat

Fig. 22(b, c)—Monasterboice high cross as pictured in *The sculptured crosses of ancient Ireland*. Note the class division in these two versions of opposing sides of the cross. The 'peasants' are depicted as resting beside the cross but paying no interest, while the 'gentry' are studying the cross intently.

the same design, proof that the Irish artists were possessed of great fertility of invention as well as ability in design and execution.

The Royal Irish Academy[14] preserves a printed notice, dated 12 October 1857 and addressed from 12, Middlesex Place, New Road [London] N.W., which states that

> Mr O'Neill is happy to be able to inform his Subscribers that his work on the Irish crosses is completed; its production has occupied a considerable time, but collecting the materials, making the drawings, and defraying the cost was a very heavy task—hence the delay.
>
> The Sixth Part has been unusually expensive. In addition to the usual amount of matter, there are the Title, an original Essay on Ancient Irish Art, and an Appendix of quotations. One of the prints is colored in order to explain Irish ornament—hence the Sixth Part has called forth an extra amount of labor and expense; to aid in defraying which, an addition of 4s. is made; the price of the Sixth Part being £1.
>
> Mr O'Neill returns his grateful thanks to his Subscribers, and begs that Post Office Orders be made payable at Paddington.

At the bottom, O'Neill has added in ink: 'Society £3 and Self £1'.

So, finally, in 1857, apparently after individual parts had earlier been issued, the time had come for the complete high crosses book to be launched upon the world, not with the title proposed in 1853 but bearing on the title-page the words

ILLUSTRATIONS OF THE MOST INTERESTING
OF
THE SCULPTURED CROSSES
OF
ANCIENT IRELAND

DRAWN TO SCALE AND LITHOGRAPHED BY

HENRY O'NEILL
LONDON
HENRY O'NEILL, 12, MIDDLESEX PLACE, NEW
ROAD, N.W.
1857

In his Introduction, which seems to have been issued separately to the 36 lithographs which make up the illustrations, O'Neill starts out by criticising earlier authors: 'the little that has been done by Irish writers about these crosses were better undone'. The remark that Mervyn Archdall in his *Monasticon Hibernicum* of 1786 made about the carvings on Muiredach's Cross at Monasterboice, Co. Louth, that they 'show the uncivilized age in which they were executed', was of the kind to make O'Neill go berserk, as it was the exact opposite of the message that he was trying to get across. Edward Ledwich, who published the first edition of his *Antiquities of Ireland* only four years after Archdall, O'Neill found simply 'erroneous'. But some of his sharpest criticism he reserved for George Petrie, who, he said, wrongly transcribed the inscription on the base of the cross at Tuam, Co. Galway, and gave the wrong height and date for it, as well as ascribing the date of the North Cross at Clonmacnois to about two centuries earlier and dating the two Monasterboice crosses (Fig. 22, b and c) to the tenth century, his reasons for doing so being 'too feeble to satisfy anyone'. Later generations would, however, give the palm to Petrie, and say that he was much closer to the mark than anything that O'Neill had to say on the subject. The height of the Tuam cross as given by Petrie was that of parts of two separate crosses mounted on top of one another, whereas O'Neill thought that the two belonged to the same cross which was missing a piece in the middle, which would have given it a height of about 30ft—a trap into which Liam Gogan fell 80 years later.[15]

O'Neill stressed that the main characteristics of Irish art were interlaced ornaments, bands, cords, serpents, dogs, birds, and even human beings. In addition, he said, there were also other modes: spirals, waves, zigzags, frets etc. He rightly pointed out that vegetal forms are very rare, but asserted that the ornaments he listed 'display wonderful powers of invention and execution, and entitle the ancient Irish to rank as the greatest masters of ornamental art that ever existed. In this opinion I stand alone, but an attentive study of every age and country has led me to this conclusion.' The praise which J.O. Westwood and even Giraldus Cambrensis had lavished on Irish manuscript illumination he wanted to have extended to the works of stone and metal. The excellence, the amazing laboriousness and perfection of these works of art indicate a very long and a very prudent cultivation. The style of all is the same—unmistakably Irish. It could not have come from Rome, as Rome never had it. It originated in Ireland, and extended thence to Great Britain and the continent of Europe. 'By giving proofs that my native land was anciently the most civilized in Europe', O'Neill continued, he hoped to 'create an interest in a fine country and a gifted people, who still retain evidence that they were once "Great, glorious and free", and that Ireland was "The Emerald gem of the western world", not alone because of her verdant soil, but because she had an advanced civilization when the rest of Europe was sunk in barbarism'. It should be said that O'Neill believed that this civilisation had its source in the prehistoric period, that the serpents on the crosses went back to heathen times and that even the form of the Irish cross was pagan.

Nowadays most would find O'Neill's views somewhat askew, but that should not prevent us from admiring his great achievement in illustrating Irish high crosses in book form for the first time, and delineating pretty accurately the details of their ornament and their figure sculpture. The size of the plates (22in. by 15in.) alone makes them impressive, and one must congratulate an artist who was prepared to go to the trouble of lithographing all of his 36 plates himself and at his own expense. Much more so than the few examples displayed at the great Dublin Exhibition on Leinster Lawn referred to earlier, his plates made the public realise for the first time just how truly interesting and varied these Irish crosses were. This is deserving of the highest praise and makes us realise that O'Neill's book is not only an artistic achievement but also one of *the* most important illustrated works on Irish archaeology (in its broadest sense)

dating from the nineteenth or even the twentieth century.

Of the crosses he illustrates, that at Dunnamaggan in County Kilkenny would probably be reckoned nowadays to date from the later medieval period, whereas all the others can be accommodated roughly in the ninth to the twelfth centuries. These fifteen crosses are reproduced in whole or in part, or both, and achieve a high degree of accuracy, though he may have had to struggle somewhat with disfigurement by lichen, which covers many of the crosses today, except those at Tuam, Moone, Durrow and Clonmacnois, which have been brought indoors in recent decades to prevent further erosion by the weather.

The first quarter of the lithographs, plates 1–9, grew out of O'Neill's work when he was living in Kilkenny in the first half of the 1850s—those same drawings which were displayed at meetings of the Kilkenny Archaeological Society, mentioned above. He devoted five separate plates to illustrations of what he called the 'Kilclispeen Crosses' and which we would now generally call the Ahenny group of crosses, even though Ahenny is in County Tipperary. It must have been the high-quality carving of geometrical ornament on the two Ahenny crosses that pleased him most and persuaded him to devote so much space to them, though he admits that he got a drawing of one side of one of the crosses from the Revd Graves. It is clear that his greatest fascination is with the interlace and geometrical ornament as found particularly on the Ahenny crosses, and he was less interested in the biblical scenes on the important scriptural crosses at Monasterboice, Clonmacnois and Ardboe (this last the only Northern Ireland cross to feature in the *High crosses* album and the only one in Ulster to survive *in situ* in its entirety).

Nevertheless, he does expend considerable effort in giving us a fairly accurate representation of the figure sculpture as it was in his day, though his details do not help us any further in elucidating some of the subject-matter of the more difficult panels, nor can his work be used specifically to demonstrate whether or how far the crosses have deteriorated in the century and a half since the book's appearance. His was also the first major attempt in modern times to make sense of the various Old and New Testament scenes on the crosses. With his Protestant background, he would have been more at home in the former than many of his Catholic contemporaries, who would, however, have been able to appreciate the New Testament material which O'Neill was revealing. While modern scholarship would suggest that O'Neill did not get the interpretation of all of the panels right, it is remarkable just how many he did. The jury is still out in certain cases and, rather than trying to think up some fanciful interpretation for some of the panels (as others have done), O'Neill was honest enough to say that he was able to recognise only a certain number of the biblical scenes carved on the crosses.

O'Neill's *Catalogue* of 1855 (mentioned above) had already brought out one feature of the crosses which he was able to illustrate dramatically in plate 35 of his high crosses book (Pl. 17), namely that the crosses must have been *coloured*. Using interlace panels from Monasterboice and elsewhere, he coloured in the various strands that make up the interlace, and showed how they only made sense as a pattern and can only be clearly understood if each of the bands is separated by being painted in a different colour. This can also be seen in his Bodleian drawings mentioned above. Even if not a trace survives on any of the Irish crosses today (as was probably the case, too, in O'Neill's day), he demonstrated that these great stone monuments were much more attractively coloured originally than their monochrome grey appearance would suggest today.

Another valuable aspect of the work was O'Neill's placing beside some of the major crosses a series of memorial stones from the cross site, a feature which applies not only to Monasterboice but more particularly to Clonmacnois, where hundreds of examples still survive today and which O'Neill had sketched on his visit in 1854. Margaret Stokes was to make up for what Graves and O'Neill saw as Petrie's dereliction of duty in not publishing these memorial stones, particularly the Clonmacnois ones, by devoting two volumes to Petrie's rubbings in 1872–8,[16] and Macalister devoted another volume to the Clonmacnois examples in 1909.[17]

A most appealing aspect of many of O'Neill's plates of the crosses is the addition of people looking at—or ignoring—the cross beside which they stand or sit, thereby providing a human scale. In the two plates of the Tall or West Cross at Monasterboice (Fig. 22(b,c)) we see two different strata of society—the top-hatted gentleman staring up in admiration of the cross, and the lower echelons more informally dressed, accompanied by a small girl, taking little or no interest in it. In some of the Kilkenny plates we have a particularly attractive collection of people—man and wife, mother and child, etc.—enlivening the scene.

O'Neill did not mind criticising others but was less receptive to criticism of his own work, of which he was—with justification—inordinately proud. Dr Frazer (a Scot, I believe) was one who was not particularly enthusiastic about the *Crosses* book, and unhelpful remarks by others rankled with the author for a long time, as we can see in a letter which O'Neill wrote to Sir John Gilbert (a vice-president of the Royal Irish Academy) in 1875, published on pages 197–8 of Rose Mulholland Gilbert's *Life of Sir John T. Gilbert* (London, 1905) as follows:

> From the time I issued the first part of my work on the Crosses till now, rumours have reached me that, being only an artist, I have produced an artistic publication, it is true, but one wanting in that accuracy which an antiquarian requires. Even the R.I. Academy has not scrupled to charge me with resorting to unworthy personalities instead of something of antiquarian value in the text of that work, and, still later, the authors of the ancient inscriptions now publishing by the Kilkenny Arch. Society have published in their prospectus the injurious assertion that the inscriptions I have published in my work, *being in perspective*, are of little value to the antiquarian—the fact being that there is only one inscription in perspective, that to the Killamery Cross, and that inscription I have given in the text. I enclose a letter from Mr Doolin respecting the correctness of my prints.
>
> I would be extremely sorry to descend to personalities against any man, and feel that the statement in the Academy's Catalogue, and that by Mr

Stokes and Dr Reeves, is not alone painful to me, but, I need hardly say, being incorrect, are unworthy of those who made them. Possibly with this you have nothing to do, but I think it may be well to place in your hands Mr Doolin's letter, as it will refute the erroneous statements respecting my prints of the Sculptured Crosses.

It may be said, in parentheses, that 'the authors of the ancient inscriptions' are presumably Petrie and his posthumous editor, Margaret Stokes, but it is somewhat disingenuous of O'Neill to say, after all his trenchant criticism of the former, particularly with regard to inscriptions, that he is not descending to personalities.

Looking, however, at the positive critique of O'Neill's *Crosses* book, it is worth noting the contents of a flyer of around 1858 (the year after actual publication), preserved among the Windele manuscripts in the Royal Irish Academy,[18] where O'Neill gives a list of approving endorsements from both press and private sources, of which the following is a selection.

> *The Ulster Journal of Archaeology*: The work could not have been undertaken by a gentleman more competent in every respect to do it justice than Mr O'Neill. With a warm—we might say enthusiastic—admiration of Ancient Irish Art, he combines antiquarian lore, artistic skill, untiring perseverance, and a style as clear and glowing as his own wonder-working pencil.

> *Art Journal* [which had been critical of some of his views, as we saw in a previous chapter]: The work is well executed, and though peculiarly deserving of Irish support, is equally deserving the attention of antiquaries of all nations.

> *Revd J. Graves* of Kilkenny: These lithographs combine the scrupulous accuracy of the antiquary with the feeling and skill of an artist.

> *Revd J. S. Porter*, Belfast: Your devotion to the noble task which you proposed to yourself, and which you have so successfully completed, is praiseworthy, or rather is above all praise.

> *Kilkenny Moderator*: Whether as pictures, as proofs of antiquarian zeal and knowledge, of accuracy, or of beautiful lithography, we fearlessly assert that his plates can claim comparison with any similar work which has seen the light in the United Kingdom; Ireland, certainly, has not seen anything like it.

> *Sir R. Colt Hoare*: Neither England nor Scotland possess such rich crosses as Ireland. The Monasterboice crosses are by far the finest examples.

> *Lord Talbot de Malahide*: I shall be happy to do anything in my power to recommend your splendid work on Irish crosses. I have made a point of doing so whenever I have had an opportunity.

O'Neill then lists the societies and institutions which have taken the work: the Committee of Council on Education (two copies); the Royal Academy; the Royal Irish Academy; the Royal Dublin Society; the Kilkenny Archaeological Society (three copies); Queen's College, Belfast, etc., adding by hand 'Trinity College, Dublin'.

One letter of 19 October 1857, from the Revd J. Scott Porter,[19] mentioned above, is worth quoting, as saying that

> I like this No. very much. The Ardboe crosses are greatly mutilated, it is true that they are carefully represented; and the coloured plate, and the view of Monasterboice are perfectly beautiful, the latter especially. I conceive that now that you have it on the stone, you might make it the commencement of a *landscape series* which would reflect honour on you, and I trust not to be altogether unprofitable. [Porter's disagreement with O'Neill's views on round towers will be quoted later (p. 85).]

Another letter will not be out of place here, coming as it does from the pen of J.O. Westwood, author of *Palaeographia Sacra Pictoria*, who writes from the Taylor Institute in Oxford on 3 April 1858[20] to say that he was saddened to read in the *Archaeological Journal* that O'Neill's work on the Irish crosses had ceased at the end of 36 plates. The subject was at least worthy of *A hundred plates* and, he continues, 'it is no compliment either to our rich antiquaries or to the gentry of Ireland who ought to have felt proud in the production of such a work that it has been allowed to cease. It was a labour of love and is one of the most important contributions to our knowledge of the fine arts in Ireland (unique as they so completely are of their kind and consequently so truly national—) no one can doubt.' Westwood then goes on to ask O'Neill for a copy of his *Catalogue of illustrations* of 1855, and also of his *Essay on the Irish crosses* as distinct from the former (obviously what is now regarded as the Introduction to the *Crosses* book itself, but originally issued separately). Westwood concludes by asking O'Neill whether he would consider disposing of his collection of rubbings of Irish crosses and inscribed stones. In a letter to James Graves from 23 Aungier Street in Dublin, dated 18 October 1853,[21] O'Neill says that he was visited by one of his correspondents, J.O. Westwood, along with A.W. Franks of the British Museum, who were 'well pleased with his rubbings' of monuments, and it may have been the latter who made the suggestion, mentioned in a further letter to Graves, of 9 November that year,[22] that he might dispose of them to the British Museum. It is unlikely, however, that O'Neill would have wanted to entertain such a suggestion, as he was incensed, years later, at having to give the British Museum a copy of his *High crosses* book for nothing, under copyright, and had to pay £40 in law costs to stave off a court case which the Museum appear to have threatened to take against him.[23] In the end, it was obviously O'Neill's widow who finally sold the rubbings, and many are among those now preserved in the Bodleian Library in Oxford.[24]

O'Neill must have expected the academic and higher levels of society to be interested in his ground-breaking work, but his letters to his Cork antiquarian friend John Windele, preserved in the Royal Irish Academy, provide a number of instances where—probably hiding his disappointment—he expresses the hope that certain influential people might obtain a copy, and he is also on record as trying to get money from subscribers in Kilkenny who had not paid up!

Despite all his efforts, however, the book was slow to sell—the price of £5 at the time probably put a lot of people off. On the back cover of his single volume on the round towers of County Dublin (see below, p. 87), which was published in 1877, twenty years after the work on high crosses first appeared, he was still advertising the book (but now at £20!), making it an attractive proposition for the bibliophile in stating that 'less than 200 copies have been printed, the stones [for the plates] have been cancelled, and a second edition will not be published'. An American edition was, however, published by A.M. Hunt of Boston in 1916, recently reproduced in an undated Kessenger Legacy reprint, which inserts the plate with the Moone Cross upside down. Furthermore, a few of the designs in the *Crosses* book were reproduced in inferior quality in a book entitled *Examples of ornament … drawn from original sources* by Fr Bedford, T. Scott, T. Macquoid and H. O'Neill, edited by Joseph Cundall and published in London in 1855, at a time when preparations for the high cross plates had not been completed.[25]

Towards the end of his life, O'Neill was well aware of the impact of his *Crosses* book on Irish society. In an 1877 appeal for money (see Chapter 12)—where he stated that he had given up his 'very remunerative' profession as a portrait painter in order to produce the *Crosses* book—he talks of the crosses, their forms and modern imitations, and his role in the popularity of the latter:[26]

> The form of the Irish cross has been accepted as the most appropriate one for a Christian monument that has ever been invented; imitations have been made in great numbers, and are erected in graveyards throughout Ireland; they have also been exported to England, and even as far as Australia. A stronger testimony to the ability of the Irish artists could hardly

be afforded than by thus adopting their designs in place of those of Greece and Rome—the stelae, sarcophagi, urns, obelisks, and other inelegant monumental forms of the classical nations.

My work has been the sole authority for these numerous imitations, a result with which I am highly gratified, but it has not been the least pecuniary advantage to myself

—a theme which, as we shall see, was subsequently taken up by no less a personage than Oscar Wilde.

It is interesting to remark that, in a notably nationalistic cemetery such as Glasnevin, it took until the 1860s before the 'Celtic cross' began to become popular as a gravestone type, and it was not really until the 1870s that O'Neill's influence began to make its mark more widely there, and elsewhere throughout the country. It is, therefore, essentially through the influence of O'Neill's work that the 'Celtic cross' became the preferred form of gravestone throughout Ireland and beyond from the second half of the nineteenth century onwards.

NOTES

1. *Journal of the Kilkenny and South-East of Ireland Archaeological Society* **2** (1) (1853), 211.
2. O'Neill to Windele from London; Royal Irish Academy 4/B/13/62(i).
3. Bearing a pencil number 683.
4. Revd James Graves, 'A list of the ancient Irish monumental stones at present existing at Clonmacnoise', *Proceedings and Transactions of the Kilkenny and South-East of Ireland Archaeological Society* **3** (1854–5), 293.
5. *Ibid.*, 291.
6. *Ibid.*
7. *Ibid.*, 296.
8. *Ibid.*, 291.
9. *Ibid.*
10. *Ibid.*, 292.
11. *Ibid.*, 292.
12. Royal Irish Academy 4/B/15/8 (ii).
13. Royal Irish Academy 54/B/20/119, November 1860.
14. Royal Irish Academy 24 O 39/JG/114 (xi).
15. L.S. Gogan, 'The famed High Cross of Tuam, mysteries of its construction solved; light on mediaeval methods in art', *The Standard*, 9 August 1930, pp 11 and 13.
16. George Petrie, *Christian inscriptions in the Irish language* (ed. M. Stokes) (2 vols) (Dublin, 1872 and 1878).
17. R.A.S. Macalister, *The memorial slabs of Clonmacnois, King's County*, extra volume of the *Journal of the Royal Society of Antiquaries of Ireland* for 1907–8 (Dublin, 1909).
18. Royal Irish Academy 4/B/18/59 (ii).
19. Sketch-book B, between pp 16 and 17.
20. Ditto.
21. Royal Irish Academy 24 O 39/JG/114 (v).
22. Royal Irish Academy 24 O 39/JG/14 (vii).
23. Royal Irish Academy 4/B/19/42.
24. MSS Top. Ireland A. 1–4 (31,862–5).
25. The crosses illustrated through ornamental details were those of Killamery, Termonfeckin, Monasterboice, Kilclispeen (Ahenny) and Kells.
26. Royal Irish Academy 12 N 23/2/73/29.

Pl. 18—*The high cross at Drumcliff, Co. Sligo.* From *The fine arts and civilization of Ireland* (1863).

7

THE FINE ARTS AND CIVILIZATION
OF ANCIENT IRELAND

O'Neill's second book (neither his *Picturesque views*, the drawing book of 1846 nor the *Catalogue* of 1855 he would apparently count as books) was *The fine arts and civilization of ancient Ireland*, published in London by Smith, Elder and Company, and in Dublin by George Herbert. The title-page indicates that it is 'illustrated with chromo and other lithographs, and several woodcuts', and the date given is 1863. It was probably the first time that chromo-lithography was used extensively in any publication on Irish archaeology (in its broadest sense); the *Sculptured crosses* had only one page of full colour, the one demonstrating that the crosses must have been painted originally.

The book is an illustrated extension of the thesis O'Neill was propounding in the Introduction to his *Crosses* book. With it, he is making the point that Irish art, rather than being downgraded by some, should be appreciated by the many, that Irish art style 'was carried to an almost miraculous degree of excellence, and the best works in that style which still remain are, for inventive power, sound principles, and masterly execution, the very finest examples of ornament that ever were executed', in addition to which it was a style that was completely national. O'Neill was certainly one of the first to demonstrate the high quality of early Irish art, though many today (and also in his day) would have found it hard to swallow when he claimed that the Irish style 'influenced the taste in Art in the civilized world, from the Baltic to the Mediterranean, and even as far east as distant Egypt'. He is astonished that a style that arose in Ireland 'attained a perfection beyond which we cannot imagine it possible to pass', and, despite the fact that it flourished for centuries, that it should be all but totally forgotten. To counteract this, he presents in his book a number of examples (listed below) which 'will gratify the national heart because they are national and glorious' and will 'improve the taste by their excellence'. He thereby becomes the premier promoter of the excellence of early Irish art in all its various facets—a sentiment which, of course, reflected the nationalistic movements which were spreading over Europe in the 1840s. O'Neill's ideas were no doubt joyously received by the more nationalistically minded in the country but may not have gone down quite so well among the academics.

The Irish style, which he termed Byzantine because it was ornamental in contrast to the more representative and image-driven sculpture of the human form among the Greeks and Romans, 'holds the pre-eminence for every quality which renders works of Art excellent, namely great originality and fertility of invention, wonderful powers of execution, combined with a profound knowledge of the principles of Art, to which we may add a thorough mastery of color or chromatic effect'.

O'Neill then presents extracts from Giraldus Cambrensis, the twelfth-century Welsh commentator on Ireland, the manuscript scholar J.O. Westwood (whom we have already encountered elsewhere commenting on O'Neill's *Crosses* book) and other largely forgotten worthies, who give a very praiseworthy account of early Irish art. This he contrasts with the negative views on the value—indeed, the very existence—of Irish civilisation before the coming of the Normans given by Brinkley and Archdall (see pp 47 and 52), which he then counterbalances with views in favour of the civilisation of ancient Ireland by the eighth-century Venerable Bede, the poets Edmund Spenser and Thomas Moore, and even by Dr Samuel Johnson.

To underline his admiration for the quality of early Irish art, he then discusses over a number of chapters various categories displaying that quality, starting with the cross at Drumcliff, Co. Sligo (Pl. 18), which he had omitted from his *Sculptured crosses* and which he illustrates with two beautiful chromo-lithographs showing each face of the cross; in addition, he provides woodcuts of the ornament on the narrow side. There follow short chapters on the sarcophagus in Cormac's Chapel in Cashel and a dolmen ('rock monument') not far from the Drumcliff cross, before O'Neill launches into a detailed description of the eleventh/twelfth-century Lismore Crozier (Pl. 19), which had been lent by the duke of Devonshire for display at the Cork exhibition of 1852. This was the first time that very detailed drawings of the rich and varied ornament of the crozier were published, most of them in colour—and reduced for publication with the aid of Mr J. Lewis's recently patented machine called 'the Automaton Pentagraph'. The same treatment was afforded to the shrine of St Patrick's Bell, which had been deposited in Trinity College, Dublin, in O'Neill's day and is now in the National Museum in Dublin. The crozier was illustrated again in the *Dublin Builder* of 15 March 1863, where the review of *The fine arts* book on page 50 contains the following paragraph:

Every Irish gentleman, whether professional or not, who feels interested in the past glories of his country, and who wishes it a prosperous future, should read Mr O'Neill's work, in which the high state of civilization of our forefathers is proved beyond doubt. Professional men, whether painters, architects, or sculptors, would do well to study the ancient ornament of their country, with a view to its reproduction as also to the formation of a style of ornament based on its principles and suited to the wants of our times. Mr O'Neill has opened up the subject for them, and has laid down principles which it would be easy to work out.

One of O'Neill's favourite pieces of metalwork was the Tara Brooch, which he illustrated here and a number of times elsewhere, using the work of London's best wood-engravers, which he admitted, even then, had failed to convey the excellence of the workmanship. Now on display in the National Museum in Dublin, it was at the time in the Victoria and Albert Museum in London, where a writer in the *Times* described it as 'more like the work of fairies than of human beings'. O'Neill was, however, unable to add colour to his decorations from some manuscripts which he discusses, most of them now in the Library of Trinity College, particularly the Books of Durrow, Kells and Armagh (Fig. 23). Interestingly, the initials he uses were taken from that same Book of Armagh and also from the Ricemarsh Psalter.

The book was very favourably reviewed at length in the *Dublin Builder* of 15 March 1863, and mentioned again in the issue of the following 1 September. An extract from the chapter on 'The Rock Monument at Drumcliff' was republished in the 1 May 1875 issue of the *Irish Builder*. The last third of the book was given over to the subject of round towers, discussed below in Chapter 11 but also reported in the *Dublin Builder* of 1 October 1863.

It is worth rounding off this brief chapter with some glowing accounts in the press of the time about the book, as quoted in the concluding pages of O'Neill's next book, *Ireland for the Irish* (see Chapter 9):

From *Saunders' Newsletter*:

The appearance of the work is greatly in its favour, binding and paper good, type good. Illustrations excellent, and as varied as good, consisting of woodcuts, chromo, and other lithographs … The volume will excite much interest, and lead to discussions in high and learned quarters in this country and in England.

The chromo-lithographs are finished with the precision and delicacy of touch and brilliance and cleanness of colour of the early artists, the objects of admiration of our artist-author. Our author holds no middle view where the character and ancient glory of his country are in question, but then he sets forth a

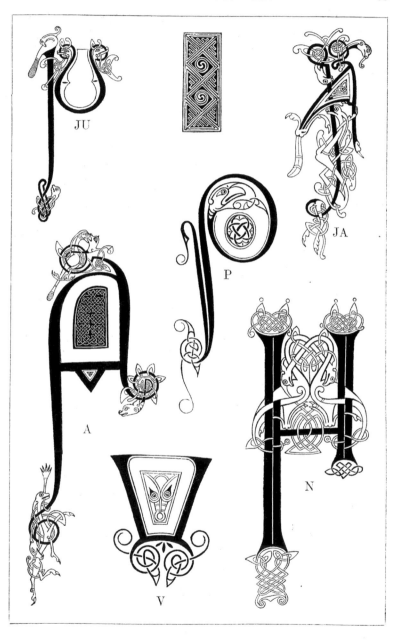

mass of interesting, undoubted facts, and gives sound or very specious reasons for all he asserts. He writes with the same mastery of language as if the pen, instead of the pencil, had occupied his fingers the greater part of his life. His country owes him gratitude for his vindication of her early skill and learning in this and his work on the Sculptured Crosses. The woodcuts display the rare skill of our countryman, Mr Hanlon, in his peculiar walk.

From the *Daily Express*:

Mr O'Neill, in his preface, expresses a hope that this work may be considered a credit to the Irish Press. It certainly will be so considered by all persons of taste. The illustrations are exceedingly beautiful; the printing is admirable; the binding is elegant; and altogether, so far as the getting up of the work is concerned, it is a model of good taste and beautiful workmanship. The style of the Author is in keeping with the artistic execution of the framework which he has chosen for his thoughts. It is correct, clear, sensible and genuine, with nothing tawdry or pretentious,—with no brilliancy but what shines out of the gems which he has set with so much skill.

Fig. 24—*Brenanstown Dolmen, Co. Dublin.*
Pen and ink drawing (Glenstal Sketch-
book G, p. 42).

8

DOLMENS AND CHURCHES

O'Neill occasionally cut out notices in the newspapers reporting finds of prehistoric burials, but his main interest in pre-Christian Ireland was in the monuments standing above ground. One would expect him to have taken a particular interest in sites like Newgrange or the passage graves on the Lough Crew Hills, also in County Meath, but there is very little on County Meath in the surviving notebooks. We can only presume that his notes and sketches on such monuments would have been contained in one of his many sketch-books which have been lost.

The area around Dublin had plenty of megalithic tombs to whet his appetite, however, and most of these he visited and avidly sketched, as seen in the Glenstal sketch-book marked G. He made a watercolour of the *Howth dolmen* with its massive toppled capstone on 9 April 1841,[1] fully twenty years before Sir Samuel Ferguson published his poem on the cromlech, with accompanying notes on early Irish art by Petrie (following O'Neill's essay in *High crosses* four years earlier) and decorative initials designed by Margaret Stokes.[2] He reckoned that the Howth capstone must have weighed between 90 and 100 tons, but no one has lifted it in the meantime to check how accurate his guess may have been! This top stone, O'Neill tells us, is called 'Fin's quoit' from a tradition that it was thrown into its present position by Finn MacCuul (his spelling!).

It was in 1840, one year before he visited Howth, that O'Neill climbed *Killiney Hill* to draw a circular enclosure 90ft in diameter with what he called 'Druidical Remains', consisting of a chair nearly 6ft high, of which he provides a sketch and a back view.[3]

On Christmas Day 1851—the same day that he visited *Puck's Castle*, mentioned above (p. 42)—O'Neill

turned his attention to visiting the dolmen at what he called *Shanganagh*,[4] otherwise known today as *Loughlinstown*. Towards the end of the preceding October he had visited the large example tucked away in a valley at *Brenanstown* (Fig. 24) near Cabinteely, where in his sketch he placed a man (himself?) admiring the weighty capstone. He also provides us with an end view 'to show how the sides of the top rock overhang the supporting stones'.

The week after Christmas that year turned out to be a busy one for O'Neill, because on 28 December he visited *Knockmaroon* in Dublin's Phoenix Park, where a prehistoric burial was marked by a flat capstone 4ft long and standing 18in. above ground level. He also noted a report in the *Transactions of the Royal Irish Academy* of 1848 about a mound—in fact the remains of a passage grave—at *Knockmany*, Co. Tyrone, and from the same year an account of the discovery of human and animal bones in a number of 'cairnes' near *Ballysadare*, Co. Sligo (*Carrowmore?*), said to be the monuments of the Fir Bolgs slain at the Battle of Moytura.

On New Year's Eve 1851 he visited *Mount Venus* in the Dublin Mountains (Fig. 25), where he made a remarkable pen and wash sketch of the dolmen there, with a boy accompanied by a dog, and a man holding a gun. The capstone, in this instance, he reckoned to be about 65 tons, and also gave his version of what it may have looked like originally—14½ft tall.

One dolmen he could not have missed out on is that at *Kiltiernan*, 'located near Golden Ball, a village near the Scalp', which he visited on 2 January 1852 (Fig. 26). The now-celebrated view of it by Beranger,[5] executed about three-quarters of a century earlier, would not have been

Fig. 25—*Mount Venus Dolmen, Co. Dublin*. Pen and wash drawing (Glenstal Sketch-book G, p. 58).

Fig. 26—*Kiltiernan Dolmen, Co. Dublin* (Glenstal Sketch-book K, unnumbered page).

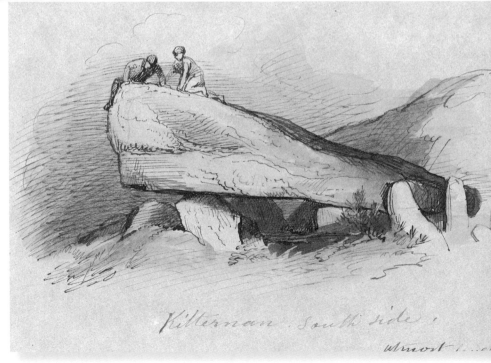

Fig. 28—A pencil drawing of the reassembled Romanesque doorway in *Kilmore Cathedral, Co. Cavan* (Glenstal Sketch-book G, p. 136).

known to O'Neill. He also visited what he calls a 'Giant's Grave' at *Ballybetagh* nearby. A local farmer, Larry Walsh, described it as being shaped like a coffin, with the broad part, 'the shoulders', at the western end. Larry, he recounts, remembered it as having been covered with two great flags, which raised a question in O'Neill's mind as to whether this was a cromlech with two roof rocks, but which modern research would now brand as a wedge-shaped gallery grave.

On the same day O'Neill visited *Glencullen*, with a capstone 10ft long and 4ft thick, of which he also provides us with a sketch. The last of his series of dolmen drawings is that of *Cloche leithe* near Rosbercon, Co. Kilkenny, discussed in the 1850 edition of the *Transactions of the Kilkenny Archaeological Society*. Its capstone he reckoned to be a mere 47 tons. On the following 1 February he was drawing a leaning pillar stone standing about 10ft high some two miles east of Kilkenny city (near the free school).

He came back to these dolmens sometime later and did some beautiful drawings for reproduction, some of which are illustrated here.[6] His interest in prehistoric monuments also extended to a stone circle at *Ballynamona*, Co. Cork (Fig. 27).

In O'Neill's appeal for assistance to prevent his becoming a pauper at the end of his life (see Chapter 12), he said that churches were one class of antiquities of which he had been a zealous student for more than half a century. Yet it is remarkable how few churches feature in the surviving sketch-books, nor do they make any significant appearance in his publications.

His fascination with various styles of masonry, including that used in churches and oratories, does emerge in the early pages of his large manuscript 'Antiquities' volume, but there, in many cases, he is copying from the works of, among others, Richard Rolt Brash and the earl of Dunraven, and even very occasionally Petrie—*Dulane*, Co. Meath, *Temple Benen* on the Aran island of Inishmore, Co. Galway, and *Leaba Molaga*, Co. Cork, being good examples. One site which grabbed his attention was *Glendalough*, Co. Wicklow, to which he would have been drawn in his country-wide survey of round towers. There he did allow himself plenty of time to look at the churches, making a plan of the *Cathedral*, and succumbing to the fascination of *Reefert* and *Trinity* churches and of 'St Kevin's Kitchen'. In the same county he did a fine drawing of the

Fig. 29—*Louth Abbey, Co. Louth*. Pencil drawing (Glenstal Sketch-book B, p. 24).

doorway of the church at *Aghowle*—one of the rare instances where a church he studied did not have a round tower near it, as was also the case at Kilmore, Co. Cavan, of which his pencil drawing survives (Fig. 28). Easy to reach from his Dundalk base was the village of *Louth*, where O'Neill drew in pencil the medieval church ruin (Fig. 29) and the roofed *St Mochta's House*. Otherwise, the later medieval abbeys or friaries seem to have had comparatively little appeal for him, an exception being *Creevelea* friary in County Leitrim, where a reference to 'see Plate' in his description would suggest that he did intend to publish his work on it. Another exception was *Clare 'Abbey'* near Ennis, Co. Clare, which he sketched in 1875. We might have expected the more impressive Ennis Franciscan friary nearby to have been included in the same trip, but its absence, and that of other Franciscan, Dominican and Cistercian foundations, are best explained either by O'Neill's lack of interest in or time to devote to them, or by his inclusion of them in one or more of the lost sketch-books. We do, however, learn of his further interest in other churches or monasteries through the pictures he exhibited, as listed in the Appendix, where Glendalough, St Canice's Cathedral in Kilkenny, the Franciscan friary at Drogheda, Adare, Co. Limerick, and Howth 'Abbey' may be added to the list.

NOTES

1. In Glenstal Sketch-book G, p. 36.
2. Sir Samuel Ferguson, *The cromlech on Howth, a poem* (London, 1861), with drawings by Margaret Stokes and notes on Celtic ornamental art by George Petrie.
3. Sketch-book G, p. 54.
4. Drawings and discussion of this and the following dolmens are to be found in Sketch-book G.
5. Royal Irish Academy MS 3 C 30, p. 45, illustrated in P. Harbison (ed.), *Beranger's views of Ireland* (Dublin, 1991), 57.
6. The dolmen drawings can be found on pp 124–30 of O'Neill's Sketch-book K in Glenstal Abbey.

9

IRELAND FOR THE IRISH—AND A SWIPE AT THE ROMAN CATHOLIC CHURCH

O'Neill's only book with political rather than artistic intent was one which he produced in 1868. A new edition was issued from his last address at 109 Lower Gardiner Street in 1880, the year of his death, and may have been intended to help his widow financially, as there is a note on the bottom of the title-page saying 'All rights reserved for the benefit of the author's widow'. Entitled *Ireland for the Irish*, it obviously represents a further radical development of the nationalistic ideas going through his mind when he was involved with Daniel O'Connell and the Young Ireland movement during the 1840s. Running to over 100 pages, the book was dedicated to Lord Stanley, an English peer who had delivered a speech in England on the Irish question earlier in the year. The dedication ends with the words: 'Erase the bitter memories of the past by simple justice. We ask no more.' This sounds like a fairly harmless supplication, but it was the beginning of a strong anti-English bias throughout the book (reminiscent of the *Art Journal* controversy of 1845) that was directed at landlordism, which he described as 'Ireland's monster evil'. He specifically says that his ire was not necessarily directed at individual landlords—possibly just as well, as they had earlier been among his clients. Some of them, he felt, had not acted unjustly or harshly, and had even been kindly, but others had acted as thorough villains. Numbering 8,500, they monopolised the land, which they held by English law, having grabbed it by the sword in earlier centuries. Some of these English landlords, O'Neill said, were not even born in Ireland and most of them did not even live there; on the whole they detested the country and its people, and their absenteeism was draining the country of its finances. Agriculture and forestry had been sadly neglected, he

continued, with high rents forcing 200,000 people to emigrate annually. Tenants had no rights (except in some Ulster cases); if they improved their holding, they were either evicted or charged higher rents. Too much power was wielded by the agents who looked after the landlords' estates and for whom, it was rumoured, 'palm oil is found an admirable lubrication'.

O'Neill castigated the English press, which deemed Ireland to be 100 years behind England (and guess who was responsible for that?) and saw the Irish people as assassins shooting Protestants from behind the hedge, because, in O'Neill's view, O'Connell's Catholic Relief Bill of 1829 had not 'cured the moral disease of the Protestant ascendancy'. It was alright for the English press to be seen encouraging insurrection in Greece and Poland but not in its own neighbouring island, and O'Neill maintained that the country was ready to burst out into open rebellion whenever there was a chance of success. He probably had in mind the 'Manchester martyrs', Allen, Larkin and O'Brien, who were executed for having killed a policeman during an attempt to rescue a Fenian prisoner in 1867.

Justice needed to be done; tenants in town and country should be relieved of injustice, and the only way to do that was to make all land into national property. His plan to do so was simple, he said. Landlords should dispose of their legal right to hold the land, and the land monopoly in Ireland would thereby be broken. He proposed that an elective body should be set up to buy, let and manage this land thus nationalised, and the proper procedures in doing all of this should be overseen and checked by a series of Land Commissioners, who should ensure that everything was done fairly. The money for the scheme would be

Fig. 30—A poor Irish family on the
roadside some years after the Famine.
Pen and ink sketch (Glenstal Sketch-
book B, unnumbered page).

advanced by the Bank of Ireland, 'for which advances shall
be security'. Through this scheme, Ireland would be for the
Irish and, 'if justice is done, the people will not trouble
themselves with that very troublesome topic, disloyalty'.

Owen Dudley Edwards[1] summed up O'Neill's book
as a fine example of pre-Davitt socialism to obtain land
reform from the Tories, and pointed out the author's
'humour and presence of mind' in using a number of
quotations from Disraeli's *Contarini Fleming*. The prime
minister's sovereign, however, can scarcely have been
amused or impressed.

In addition to landlordism, one of O'Neill's pet
aversions was the Roman Catholic Church. Upside down
to the main text in Glenstal's Sketch-book B we find a
drawing in blue ink of a poor Catholic family huddled
together (Fig. 30), and another of a hovel near which he
may have seen them (Fig. 31). He may have intended to
publish the accompanying text as a newspaper or journal
article. Written in Kilkenny in 1852, it begins with a
complaint about the Romanists building large new
buildings for themselves at the expense of the poorest
members of the Catholic community, from whom they had
elicited alms to build these structures. O'Neill goes on to
contrast the poor quality of Catholic sermons when
compared to those of Episcopalians.

On Ash Wednesday in Kilkenny he sees women
wearing ashes who get so cold that they go into one of the
city's many 'dram shops' and get drunk, as they are not
allowed to put milk in their tea during Lent. The women
are then brought before the mayor (who is the proprietor
of one such 'dram shop') and have a fine imposed upon
them, and O'Neill believes that the wealthier citizens are
usually the owners of such shops, of which every third shop
in the town is one. He goes on to complain about the

Fig. 31—A one-roomed hovel in a pen
and ink drawing, dated 18 May 1851
(Glenstal Sketch-book B, unnumbered
page).

deficiency of intellectual societies in the town, though one—the Literary and Scientific Institute of Kilkenny—had recently been established; he retained its foundation document in his archive.[2] One priest, a Fr Rowan, reported that the communication of knowledge was too important to be left to a group of people of heterogeneous views—in other words, only the priests should be the teachers of the people. Another even condemned the new society off the altar; in O'Neill's view, this showed the Catholic clergy carrying out the dictates of the primate, Paul Cullen, which he quotes *in extenso*, commenting that Cullen had said that the pope had decided to condemn the system of mixed education.

NOTES
1. Owen Dudley Edwards, 'Oscar Wilde and Henry O'Neill', *The Irish Book* **1** (1959–62), 12.
2. Unnumbered page in Glenstal Sketch-book B.

Moiry Castle, C? Armagh
H. O'Neill

10

IRISH CASTLES—II:
LOUTH AND ADJACENT COUNTIES

We last came across O'Neill's drawings and descriptions of castles in the 1840s, and particularly in the early 1850s. We then have a gap of almost a decade and a half before we pick up his traces again on the same trail, this time in the Glenstal sketch-book marked B. While he certainly was distracted from his castle-huntings by producing some of the books discussed in previous chapters, it is very likely that the lost volumes of his sketch-books contained further material on castles about which we know nothing. All we can do is content ourselves with the material we have.

In the meantime, O'Neill had founded a family and moved with them to Dundalk, where he was to spend most of the rest of his life. He used the town as a base for his sketching activity and, at what we would now regard as pensionable age (though he, poor man, had none, as we shall see in a later chapter), he picked up his pen and paper and started off (as far as we can see) in sketching *Cooley Castle* on 21 May 1865, though it was little more than a mass of tumbled walls. As was the case with Cork and Tipperary, he went into considerable detail in discussing this castle and others that he was to visit not only in Louth but also in Armagh, Monaghan and Meath.

In 1867 we find him visiting *Balregan Castle*, about two miles south-west of the town, where he made a pencil sketch and wrote a description of the imposing but sadly demolished gateway entrance (Fig. 32), all that remained of a walled court. This had been mentioned by Thomas Wright in his *Louthiana* of 1748, a book with which O'Neill must have been familiar and which would have guided him to whichever of the county's castles he felt he should visit. On 22 May we find him at *Haynestown Castle*, the plan of which shows it to have irregular circular towers at each corner, but

these were in fact additions to what was once a very small structure indeed.

In the midst of all these tower-houses, we find O'Neill back in Kilkenny drawing the partial shaft of a high cross at *Leggettsrath*, only a mile or so outside the city. Then it is back to *Seatown* in the middle of Dundalk, which, as O'Neill sagely noted, 'is not a castle but an ecclesiastical tower, possibly the central tower of a church such as would divide the aisle from the chancel'.

Castle Roche (Pl. 22) dominates the landscape a few miles north-west of Dundalk, and there O'Neill drew two different versions of the castle; one is in Henry McDowell's collection and the other in the museum in Dundalk, the details of the foreground differing somewhat in each case. It is one of the few instances where we have watercolour (rather than monochrome) views of castles. Another, not far away and just over the border into County Armagh, is *Moyry* or *Moiry Castle* (Pl. 20), which O'Neill described in detail over eleven pages, sketched a number of times and even made a watercolour of it for sale, which is now in the collection of Mrs Cróine Magan. The following pages in the sketch-book are then taken up with newspaper clippings from the *Freeman's Journal* about the Tara Brooch and an article in the *Weekly Times* of 19 May 1869 on the subject of serpent worship. This would have been of interest to O'Neill in conjunction with his belief that serpents are present on the high crosses; furthermore, he cut out a review of a book on serpent worship in the *Weekly Times* of 9 May 1869 and pasted it into one of his own sketch-books. He did, however, ask himself the question as to whether, if serpents were found on Irish crosses, they can have originated in a land where no serpent is found.

Pl. 21—*Two sheep relaxing on a grassy slope*,
dated 29 May 1871 (Henry McDowell
collection).

Pl. 22—The impressive *Castle Roche, Co.*
Louth (Henry McDowell collection).

Back to castles again on 29 June 1867, this time to *Athclare*, a mile south of Dunleer; O'Neill drew its decorative fireplace (Fig. 33), as well as making a nice pencil sketch of the castle and the house that was built up against it (Fig. 34).

The order of castles in Sketch-book B is not necessarily that in which O'Neill visited the castles, because the next batch are spread over three years, going as far forward as 1870 and then going back to 1867. He sketched and made a plan of *Dunmahon Castle*, about three miles south of Dundalk, on 8 May 1869. Then he was in County Armagh on 9 August to sketch *Ardgonnell Castle*, which may have been a Planter structure to judge by its rather Scottish-looking turret, though Sir Phelim O'Neill is said to have been the last to live in it, in 1641. Not far away, and in the same county, is *Criffcairn Castle* (Fig. 35), of which he made an attractive pencil sketch on the same day, when he had probably already entered the eighth decade of his life. Then we revert back to 4 July 1867 for a visit to *Ma(g)hernacloy Castle* (Fig. 36) in County Monaghan, which he drew. This was followed by *Newstone Castle*, Co. Meath; its cluster of ruined buildings made it difficult for O'Neill to make an accurate plan, though he did manage to make a pencil sketch of it. The big urban castle in the town of *Ardee* he sketched on 8 July 1867, and the next castle he visits— *Ballug Castle* (Fig. 37), between Dundalk and Carlingford—brings us back full circle to 28 May 1865. He also did a drawing of *Taaffe's Castle* in Carlingford (Fig. 38), a general view of the town (Fig. 39) and the Dominican abbey, before finishing the castle series, surprisingly, at *Tybroughney Castle* in County Kilkenny, which, however, bears no date.

★★★

Judging by the above, and by the earlier chapter on castles, it is clear that O'Neill must have had it in his mind for over 40 years to write a book on Irish castles. Had he done so, it would have preceded Harold G. Leask's book—produced by the Dundealgain Press—by well over half a century. But it was never to be; in Maurice Craig's phrase, used in a different context, 'it never came to the birth'. Age, not of the castles but of the author, may well have been the reason. He left it too late; by the time he had collected all the material he wanted or needed, he was over 70 and not in good health. It was probably only at that stage that he got down to organising his thoughts on the subject, which we find in the 'Irish Castles' notebook in the Glenstal Abbey collection.

On the inside front cover he starts listing the 'appropriators' of a kind which he presumed were those who would be attacking the castles he was going to be writing about:

Banditty
Brigands
Depraved persons
Enemies
Freebooters
Graspers
Housebreakers
Invaders
Marauders
Minions of the Moon [!]
Outlaws
Rogues
Rovers
Robbers
Vagabonds

In the main part of the notebook, he begins by musing on quotations from the Psalms which he could use in chapter headings:

'I have considered the days of old, the years of ancient time' (Ps. 77.5)
'I remember the days of old' (Ps. 143.5)
'Is this your joyous city whose antiquity is of ancient days?' (Ps. 23.7)

Then, as a reminder to himself, he summarises how he intends to circumscribe the castles he wants to discuss:

Fig. 32—The vanished gateway of *Balregan Castle, Co. Louth*, a pencil drawing of the later 1860s (Glenstal Sketch-book B, unnumbered page).

Fig. 33—A decorative fireplace in *Athclare Castle, Co. Louth* (Glenstal Sketch-book B, unnumbered page).

Fig. 34—*Athclare Castle, Co. Louth*. Pencil drawing of 29 June 1867 (Glenstal Sketch-book B, unnumbered page).

CHARACTERISTICS OF SMALL CASTLES

Plan. How built. How lighted, heated, means for cooking, sleeping, cleanliness, for storing goods, scullery, water, for security against burglers or other invaders.

Situation. Plan, as square, oblong, parallelogram, with a turret on the ground floorplan, with two turrets or more, with square turrets, with round turrets.

He then launches into the purpose of his investigations:

By examining the Irish Castles, we will learn the way the gentry dwelt some few centuries back, and be able to understand what must have been the state of society when such buildings were a necessity. Castles as dwelling places were erected so late as the second quarter of the seventeenth century, 1628, about two and a half centuries back.

In estimating their former, and present declining, numbers, he remarks:

I doubt if any country in the world so abounds in castles as Ireland; there are many hundreds, perhaps some thousands, and there have been a considerable number pulled down, while in the natural course of events, there is a danger of others disappearing shortly, unless due care be taken.

Inserting a paragraph describing 'a country mansion of the present day even when the proprietor is but moderately wealthy', having many apartments with an ample supply of good furniture, breakfast parlour and drawing-room, ten or twelve fireplaces throughout the house, and decorated with

Criffcairn Castle s. Wude
Cº Armagh - 9.8.70.

pictures, he continues:

> In comparing these fortified masses of stone with country residences which are built now, the differences are indeed remarkable; now commodiousness and comfort are the primary considerations; in the castle building era, security was so imperative a necessity that, to it, all other requirements had to be relinquished.

Under the grand heading *Irish castles*, his introductory note reads:

In Ireland there are thousands of castles [which] have evidently been constructed for different purposes and at different periods. I will, in a slight way, classify them in groups:

Military castles
Strongly fortified and extensive residences of the owners of large landed property
Strongly-built houses where the ground floor windows are very narrow, but higher up there are good-sized ones.

Fig. 35—*Criffcairn Castle, Co. Armagh.* Pencil drawing (Glenstal Sketch-book B, unnumbered page).

Fig. 36—*Maghernacloy Castle, Co. Monaghan*, drawn on 4 July 1867 (Glenstal Sketch-book B, unnumbered page).

Fig. 37—*Ballug Castle, Co. Louth*, after a pencil drawing of 28 May 1865 (Glenstal Sketch-book B, unnumbered page).

Fig. 38—*Taaffe's Castle, Carlingford, Co.*
Louth (Glenstal 'Antiquities' volume,
unnumbered page).

Fig. 39—*The town of Carlingford, Co. Louth.* Pencil drawing (Glenstal 'Antiquities' volume, unnumbered page).

He gives an extensive list of examples for each category, including some not in the surviving sketch-books, and he separates out a category of structures built for the clergy, though often little different from those built by laymen (again with examples):

> Indeed, so strong was the taste for the warlike forms of structure that we find the Church (militant) embattling their churches with the creneilles and embrasures which properly were only suitable for the dwellings of laymen constructed as defences against attacks in a badly regulated country.

For one section he decides to confine himself to castles 'which we may suppose to have been built for gentry of but moderate incomes or, at least, who were beneath the powerful aristocracy in wealth and power', giving a detailed description of *Grenan Castle*, Co. Kilkenny, and other examples elsewhere. Unless such castles were high—and such is not always the case—there was but scanty accommodation, a point O'Neill confirms by comparing the space in these castles with that of the house of a 'country gentleman, of a rector, or a parish priest'. Such castles, he surmises, must have been expensive to build and

> would have cost at least as much as a comfortable roomy and healthy country residence in the brick and lath and plaster style of the present day.

He continues with mentions of urban castles—some disappeared, some still standing—and then gives us a list of dated castles (with which modern estimates would not necessarily entirely agree). Finally, returning to categories of castles which he had already given, he adds a few more and gives examples (too long to include here), showing again that he visited more castles than are described and sketched in the surviving sketch- and notebooks:

> Castles with houses or signs of attached houses
> House-shaped
> With turrets or other parts of a circular form
> With large windows
> With outworks
> With passages and rooms in the wall
> Circular Castle
> With plan in the simple shape of a parallelogram
> With two turrets in the plan
> With four turrets in the plan

. . . And there O'Neill abruptly ends his discourse on castles, never to return to it, and so we, too, must leave him and his survey of castles, with regret that he did not get around to completing the work on it earlier, leaving the world bereft of what would have been not only the first but probably also the most comprehensive single work on Irish castles. With his strength ebbing away gradually during the course of the 1870s, it must have been a cause of great pain to O'Neill that the fruits of his four-decade-long study of Irish castles would never see the light of day.

11

ROUND TOWERS

Much of the last third of O'Neill's *Fine arts of ancient Ireland* (Chapter 7) is taken up with the question of the origin and uses of the Irish round towers—a subject on which he had been brooding for decades, his first offerings to the exhibitions of the Royal Hibernian Academy having included a view of *Clondalkin round tower* in 1835.

In the book, he goes into considerable detail in descriptions of a selection of the 40 or so towers that he had visited, starting with *Kilkenny* (details of which, and an early photograph of the top, can be found in his notebooks). We are fortunate that a lovely illustration survives somewhere of this Kilkenny tower, with St Canice's Cathedral in the background, signed and dated 1850. It is reproduced here as Pl. 24, which is based on a print kindly supplied by Michael O'Dwyer of Kilkenny. O'Neill continued with *Devenish*, Co. Fermanagh, *Drumcliff*, Co. Sligo, and *Old Kilcullen*, Co. Kildare. He then lists the various theories about the use of the round towers which had earlier been current, and which are worth recording here:

1 That the Phoenicians erected them for fire temples.
2 That the Druids used them as places from which to proclaim the Druidical festivals.
3 That they were for astronomical purposes.
4 That they were Phallic emblems (This is O'Brien's theory).
5 That they were for good people, like Simon Stylites, to shut themselves up in.
6 That they were for bad people to be shut up in, till, by doing penance, they became good.
7 That they were for belfries.

8 That they were keeps, or monastic castles, to keep the clergy and their treasures in; and lastly
9 That they were beacons, or watch-towers.

To which O'Neill adds, in one of his rare jocose utterances:
And, as if nine were not enough, some wicked wag has had the cruelty to inflict a tenth theory, namely, that these towers were built by the Ancients for the purpose of puzzling the Moderns; and, alas! This has proved to be the truest theory of all; for, with all this variety the antiquarian knot is still untied; the Irish riddle is still unsolved; the moderns are puzzled.

The round tower controversy had, indeed, raged among his 'Moderns' throughout the first two thirds of the nineteenth century, and was not satisfactorily laid to rest until after O'Neill died, as a discussion in the *Irish Builder* of 1881 testifies. Against the utterers of the various theories, O'Neill's vitriol was mainly directed at George Petrie—a constant refrain both in his publications and in his private correspondence, particularly with the Cork antiquary John Windele. Almost 30 years before he published his *Fine arts* book, O'Neill had been cooperating with Petrie in the *Landscape and coast scenery* book published by Wakeman in 1835 (see p. 3). His animosity towards Petrie may already have begun to form in the aftermath of a review of the book on page 609 of the *Dublin University Review* of that year (see p. 5), in which the reviewer with the pseudonym of Anthony Poplar regretted that, in the first part of the book to be issued (the illustrations were to be brought out in monthly parts), O'Neill had spoiled the view of the Vale of Avoca (given as Ovoca), whereas Petrie's contributions

Pl. 23—*The round tower in Clondalkin, Co. Dublin*, from *The round towers of County Dublin* (1877).

were eagerly awaited in the second part.

The enmity continued when Petrie was awarded a prize for an essay on round towers (after two earlier essays on the subject by other authors, who had also won prizes) and O'Neill expressed his annoyance that it had taken thirteen years for the Royal Irish Academy to publish Petrie's essay on round towers and other structures in a form very different from what it had been when submitted for the prize in 1833. He fulminated further that, for the essay's greatly augmented form, Petrie had been awarded the substantial sum of £900, of which £725 went into Petrie's own pocket. Furthermore, although Petrie had stated that a second volume (otherwise referred to as a third part) was needed 'to contain some important proofs and facts', O'Neill castigated the Academy for not having insisted on its publication, despite Petrie's alleged commitment to publish it.

In order to take pot-shots at Petrie's views, he lists the latter's theories as follows:

1 That the towers are of Christian and ecclesiastical origin, and were erected at various periods between the fifth and thirteenth centuries.
2 That they were designed to answer, at least, a twofold use, namely to serve as belfries, and as keeps, or places of strength, in which sacred utensils, books, relics, and other valuables were deposited, and into which ecclesiastics to whom they belonged could retire for security in case of sudden predatory attack.
3 That they were, probably, also used when occasion required, as beacons or watch-towers.

In his *Fine Arts* book (see Chapter 7), O'Neill then spends a whole chapter pointing out Petrie's mistakes, starting with the statement that the doorway generally faces east but is also sometimes facing north-east or south-east. In his big 'Antiquities' manuscript notebook he produces an interesting circular diagram demonstrating the various directions in which the doorways faced. O'Neill stoutly rejected Petrie's view that the towers were Christian in

origin, and held that where a cross is found in a few instances above the door of such a tower it is not a Christian cross. Ten years earlier, however, in an article on the round tower in *Aghaviller*, Co. Kilkenny,[1] he had already started attacking Petrie in public on the subject of round towers, and got support outside the capital. On 30 December 1862 he wrote to John Windele, expressing his gratification that this Cork friend approved of the *Fine arts* chapter on 'Petrie's mistakes',[2] while Windele[3] spoke of 'the sheer impudence' of Petrie in saying that none of the south Munster antiquarians were present at the excavation of the round tower in *Cloyne*, as every one of them was present except for Windele himself. But O'Neill's persistent attacks on Petrie gradually turned Dublin's academic establishment against him, with Dean Graves, his former pupil, who was at the time the president of the Royal Irish Academy and a friend of Petrie's, refusing to take a copy of the *Fine arts* book. In a letter to Windele of 28 January 1862,[4] O'Neill wrote from Vavasour Square in Dublin complaining that 'the Petrieites are against me and a strong party here'.

O'Neill thought that he had many proofs to support Henry O'Brien's theory that the towers were phallic emblems. In the Introduction to the *High crosses* book he stated that 'O'Brien's theory best solves the question as to the origin of the Irish Pillar towers. That theory is, that they were priapic, raised in honour of the Creator who was symbolised by the image of the re-productive member of man.' He promised to write on the subject of O'Brien's views at leisure but never did so. Perhaps not surprisingly, there were independent commentators who disagreed with him, including the Revd J. Scott Porter (mentioned in an earlier chapter, p. 55), who in a letter to O'Neill,[5] whose genius he admired in producing the *Crosses* book, nevertheless took issue with him on his views on round towers. 'Why do you adopt such wild theories as to *pre*-patrician art in Ireland—serpent worship, phallic emblems and the like? … Your historical line is as deficient as your artistic excellence is conspicuous.'

Near the end of his life O'Neill finally began what was intended to be the first of many volumes illustrating the round towers, namely one confining itself to those in County

Fig. 40—The village of *Lusk, Co. Dublin*, when thatch was the most common form of roofing (Glenstal 'Antiquities' volume, unnumbered page).

Pl. 24 (opposite page)—The round tower and St. Canice's Cathedral, Kilkenny, by Henry O'Neill, signed and dated 1850. Illustration kindly provided by Michael O'Dwyer, present whereabouts of original unknown.

St Canice Kilkenny
W. O'Neill 1850

Dublin. In his notebooks we find some black-and-white versions of what were later to become the attractively coloured illustrations of his round towers volume, followed by a text, both of which appeared in 1877, three years before O'Neill's death. The towers illustrated are those at *Clondalkin*, *Lusk* (Fig. 40), *Rathmichael* and *Swords*, giving details of the doorways of *Clondalkin* (Pl. 23) and *Lusk*. These latter were reproduced in black and white in the *Irish Builder* of 15 June 1881, together with brief descriptions and an announcement that 'a biographical memoir of Mr O'Neill is likely to appear soon' —which, of course, it never did, leading to the necessity of producing the present volume to make good the lacuna. The arguments put forward by O'Neill versus Petrie were rehearsed again in a pair of articles entitled 'An inextinguishable architectural controversy' in the *Irish Builder* of 1 September and 15 September 1877. The eighth and final illustration in the Dublin *Round towers* volume gave details of cross-sections etc. of the Dublin towers.

This was, indeed, to be O'Neill's last contribution on the subject, in the text of which he reiterated his previous views about the pagan origin of the round towers and complained about Petrie's theories, though Petrie had been dead for more than a decade at the time. But Petrie won the debate hands down for all that, as subsequent scholarship has endorsed his Christian origin for the round towers with acclaim. O'Neill's continued insistence on the pagan origin of the towers has done his reputation no good and, in the eyes of the modern interested public, has consigned him to an oblivion which he may have deserved for his round tower views but which is totally undeserved in relation to his high crosses and other artistic work. He may not have been quite as good a watercolourist as Petrie but he does not deserve to have been forgotten as much as he has been.

NOTES

1. *Proceedings and Transactions of the Kilkenny and South-East of Ireland Archaeological Society* **2** (1853), 352–3.
2. Royal Irish Academy 4 /B/ 22/87.
3. Royal Irish Academy 4/B/13/62c.
4. Royal Irish Academy 4/B/23/13.
5. Sketch-book B, between pp 16 and 17.

Fig. 41—'*Oscar Wilde as a lad*', ascribed to Henry O'Neill. From Richard Harborough Sherard's *Life of Oscar Wilde* (London, 1906).

12

O'NEILL, OSCAR WILDE AND WILLIAM GLADSTONE

Understandably, in his late 70s O'Neill's energy was beginning to flag, and we find him no longer going out castle-hunting or even trying to finish his proposed book on the subject. Other than old age, one reason for this was that his health was declining. In a letter of 6 May 1897 to Sir John Gilbert,[1] the great archivist and historian of Dublin, O'Neill's widow Juliet revealed just how sick he had been for years:

In the *Freeman's Journal* there is an account of the meeting of the Royal Irish Academy, where you so kindly mentioned Mr Henry O'Neill's work on the 'Irish Crosses', and the assistance I gave him. Only for my exertions, he could not, through illness, have brought out his last three books, as I had to support the family for years. I am now sixty-six, and yours is the first public recognition of his struggles for the good of his country I have heard of in all these years, and I feel deeply touched.

The same letter, written a decade and a half after O'Neill's death, demonstrated his widow's continuing bitterness against members of the Royal Irish Academy, complaining about Dr Frazer's having said that O'Neill's work on crosses was not reliable, and adding:

To show you the party he had against him—when I took a copy of the 'Fine Arts' to Sir William Wilde, he said he, Dr William Stokes, and a number of other Academicians, had made up their minds not to buy the book; but as he was 'always gallant to the ladies', he took one from me.

Impervious to Wilde's less than lukewarm attitude, in March 1869 O'Neill could still write him a letter, preserved among the T.G. Wilson/William Wilde papers in the Royal Irish Academy,[2] hoping that Wilde would support him in becoming the illustrator of Irish antiquities, an idea apparently prompted by the discovery of the Ardagh chalice and brooches the previous year. He states that he had sent a book of his published studies to Mr Clibborn at the Academy and that he had other drawings, but the government had bought them.[3] He suggests that he would be capable of drawing the antiquities, something which he believes should be done in Ireland—work too important to 'get into foreigner's hands'.

What brought out O'Neill's antagonism to Wilde, and vice versa, was O'Neill's attacks on Petrie. Relations must, however, have been amicable for a while around 1866, when Sir William Wilde appears to have commissioned O'Neill to do a portrait of his twelve-year-old son Oscar. This we learn from page 109 of Ramsay Colles's book *In castle and court house, being reminiscences of thirty years in Ireland* (London, no date), where he says:

The original chalk head, I may mention, was done by Henry O'Neill, a well-known portrait-painter, to whom [Oscar] Wilde paid a kindly tribute in his letter to me.

In a well-researched article entitled 'Oscar Wilde and Henry O'Neill' in *The Irish Book*, Vol. 1 (1959–62)—a Dolmen Press publication—Owen Dudley Edwards (to whom I owe the reference to the Colles book) expressed the opinion that the evidence made it likely that Henry O'Neill was the author of the drawing of the young Oscar (Fig. 41) published in Robert Harborough Sherard's *The life of Oscar Wilde* (London, 1906; 3rd edn 1911), opp. p. 112, bearing the caption 'Oscar

Wilde as a lad (from a red chalk drawing)'.[4]

The acquaintance between portraitist and youthful sitter was to lead many years later to Oscar's doing his best to ameliorate the penury of the ageing painter. It came about in 1877, when O'Neill issued an impassioned *Appeal for pecuniary aid from HENRY O'NEILL, artist, author of "The sculptured crosses of ancient Ireland," "The fine arts and civilization of ancient Ireland," and other works.*[5] Written from his final address at 109 Lower Gardiner Street in Dublin, it starts off with a pitiable account of his present situation:

I am unfortunately in great pecuniary difficulties. Under these circumstances I am reluctantly compelled to apply to those who have means for assistance.
My deplorable state has not been brought on by any neglect or misconduct of mine, for I have been active, industrious and temperate, but a number of adverse circumstances have pressed against me for several years. I have been suffering from severe illness.

Furthermore, he says, he had tried many doctors, among whom only Dr Fleming (who contributes a letter to the end of the *Appeal*) was able to save his life, in addition to which he had dislocated both hands permanently and got a nasty head wound when walking down from Rathdrum Station on a dark night. He continues that he is verging on 80 years of age (which would put his birth date at 1798 and not 1800), and

am not able to earn a support for myself and family, and many years of illness have exhausted my savings. Enfeebled by ill-health, disabled by accident, sunk in debt, there is now no prospect before me but pauperism, unless promptly aided by the benevolent.
Yet I trust I have deserved better than this sad fate.

And then O'Neill goes on to relate why he deserves support:

For more than half a century I have been a zealous student of Irish antiquities, of churches, castles, round towers, and other remains of distant ages. I have gone through vast labour, fatigue, and privation in travelling over Ireland when engaged in my investigations; but I have persevered unflinchingly, and have amassed a large quantity of materials relative to the remains of ancient times.

He then summarises the views he expressed in the *Catalogue* of 1855, the essay on Irish art as the introduction to his *Sculptured crosses* and the text of *Fine arts and civilization*, and stresses the importance of his work on the development of imitations of crosses as gravestones, which 'has not been the least pecuniary advantage to myself'.

The last paragraph of the *Appeal* may be quoted here in full:

As I have laboured so long and so zealously, and also so successfully, in vindicating the character of Ancient Ireland from the errors of other Irish antiquaries who have described the ancient Irish as the vilest savages; as I have brought out unaided the finest books on Irish antiquities that have ever been published; as I have in these publications improved the national taste by the excellent examples I have selected; as I have created a new branch of skilled industry in Ireland—the imitations of sculptured crosses;—as I have vindicated the character of my country from the calumnies which have been published against it—I venture to hope that what I have done, what I have suffered, and the distressed circumstances in which I am placed, will induce those who are blessed with the means to assist me in my great necessity.

Oscar Wilde was obviously in receipt of the *Appeal* (perhaps the very copy preserved among the Wilde family papers presented to the Royal Irish Academy by T.G. Wilson in 2006) and, sympathising with the plight of the artist, sent a copy of it to *Saunders's Newsletter*, which printed it in its issue of 29 December 1877 with a long—unsigned—eulogy that is worthwhile quoting here in full:

There is something particularly sad in this simple story

of a very noble but unfortunate life. Mr O'Neill has not, in any way, over-rated either the beauty or the influence of his work. The 'Sculptured Crosses of Ancient Ireland' must always rank among the very first productions of modern Irish art. The pictures of the various crosses are not only perfectly accurate, even in the minutest detail of ornamentation, but are drawn with that sympathy and love and humility which are the three great essentials of the work of the true artist. And of the delicacy and carefulness of Mr O'Neill's pencil we can give no better proof, to those who have not seen his books, than the fact that Mr Ruskin, whose flawless and exquisite taste is so well known, paid as much as fifty guineas some years ago, for a small collection of his drawings. Of Mr O'Neill's practical influence we can give no better example than the great change which has taken place in our funeral art, since the publication of his book. Everywhere in our cemeteries there are now to be seen stately and graceful Irish crosses, which are suitable memorials of our dead, not merely as being Christian emblems, but as the works of native hand and brain. These beautiful crosses have quite displaced the urns and sarcophagi, formerly so common; emblems which were meaningless, since we neither burn nor embalm our dead, and inartistic, as being unsuited to the material and climate. Ill-health, however, the fatal apathy of the public in appreciating genius, and the narrow jealousy of an antiquarian clique, have brought Mr O'Neill, in his old age, to his present penury and distress. It remains for the Irish public to make reparation for past injustice. Ireland is under a debt to Henry O'Neill. He has benefitted his country, in rescuing her from the imputation of barbarism in early ages, and he has a right to ask for assistance.

And more than this, Mr O'Neill's case is not merely one calling for private charity; his great merits, as an antiquary and an artist, ought to be recognised by our Royal Irish Academy. This body is now in possession of a sum of £2,600, being interest and principal of a sum of £1,000 left to it by Mr Timothy Cunningham, in 1789: 'to be disposed of in such premiums as it should

think proper, and for the improvement of natural knowledge and other objects of their institution'. Out of this sum a few medals and a few prizes for essays have been awarded; but an application was lately made to the Lord Chancellor by the Academy Council to permit them to devote some of this fund to defray the expenses of the publication of their transactions. We would suggest that from this money £100 be presented to Mr O'Neill as a token of his services to antiquarian art, and to relieve his distress; and that a second £100 be given to enable him to bring out his great work on the Round Towers of Ireland, one part of which has already appeared, the remaining being unpublished for want of funds. This, we conceive, would be a disposition totally in accordance with the wishes of the founder, and a just though a somewhat tardy recognition of the labours of a great Irish antiquarian artist. Pending this, however, we trust that those who have any appreciation of an unselfish and patriotic life will not refuse to give assistance to Mr O'Neill in his distress. Among those who have already responded to Mr O'Neill's appeal are the Duke of Leinster and Sir Arthur Guinness, names ever foremost in all charitable works, Sir Bernard Burke, Mr Prendergast, Rev. Ulick Burke and many others, who are well known for their patronage of literature and their love of art.

The *Nation*, with which Oscar's mother, 'Speranza', was closely associated, also printed the Appeal and the same remarks a fortnight later, this time over the name of Oscar Wilde, which thus provides proof of his authorship. To this text was appended a letter forwarded to the newspaper by the Revd Canon U.J. Bourke, president of St Jarlath's College in Tuam, as having appeared previously in the *Tuam News*:

Hawarden, Dec. 27th, 1877

Very Revd. and Dear Sir,—Since I had the honour to accept the work you so kindly presented to me, I have received an appeal on behalf of Mr Henry O'Neill, to which I perceive your name is attached; and I have pleasure in sending a couple of pounds as a small contribution to the fund raised on his behalf. Although my acquaintance with the works of ancient Irish architecture is incomplete, yet it inspires me with a sense of high value belonging to the services of those who have laboured, like Mr O'Neill, in studying and in making known its remarkable beauties.

Very Rev. sir, your faithful and obedient
W.E. GLADSTONE

The Wilson/Wilde material in the Academy[6] also contains the 'List of Subscribers to Relieve Mr O'Neill'. Some of the top subscribers, though with Oscar's name curiously absent, may be summarised as follows:

£10   Marcus Kane of Ennis and the Duke of Westminster
£5   Mr Baron Fitzgerald, Sir Arthur Guinness
£3   Sir Bernard Burke [Ulster King of Arms]; Thomas A. Wise of London; J.O. Westwood, Oxford; Miss Cane of Celbridge
£2   J.P. Prendergast, Author of "The Cromwellian Settlement" [actually 2 guineas]; His Grace the Duke of Leinster; P.J. Keenan of the National Education Board; John Lentaigne, Dublin Castle; the Hon. W.E. Gladstone (per Rev. Canon Bourke) and the O'Conor Don of Clonetis [sic]

Many others contributed lesser sums, the total of which amounted to £82.20, so that it can be said that O'Neill benefited palpably well from the generosity of his admirers, high and low—but Wilde did not succeed in getting the Academy to give O'Neill anything from the Cunningham Fund.

One further piece of evidence showing Oscar Wilde's appreciation of the work of Henry O'Neill is found in an undated letter he wrote from No. 1 Merrion Square to Sir John Gilbert, which is reproduced on page 233 of Rosa Mulholland Gilbert's *Life of Sir John T. Gilbert* as follows:

In the *Saunders* of yesterday you will find a short article by me on the unfortunate author of the 'Irish Crosses'. I have put forward your point about the Cunningham Bequest as strongly as I could without being rude. I have just suggested it. I hope that the Academy will do something for this very learned and clever artist.

Pray offer Miss Gilbert my best wishes for the New Year, and accept them yourself, from

Yours very truly
Oscar Wilde

Oscar Wilde's comment about 'the jealousy of an antiquarian clique' in his letter to *Saunders's Newsletter* of 1877 quoted above, when taken in conjunction with the remark (p. 89) that his father and Dr William Stokes were among the Academicians who were not prepared to buy a copy of *The fine arts*, could suggest that Oscar did not approve of his recently deceased father's antagonism towards O'Neill.

NOTES
1. Rosa Mulholland Gilbert, *The life of Sir John T. Gilbert* (London, 1905), 383.
2. Reference number 12 N 23/1/45, to which Clare Lanigan kindly drew my attention.
3. The question arises: where are these drawings now, and what were they of?
4. My thanks to Helen McGinley, in the Early Printed Books section of the Library of Trinity College, Dublin, for organising a copy of the portrait for me.
5. The Royal Irish Academy preserves a copy in the T.G. Wilson/William Wilde collection presented by T.G. Wilson in 2006, bearing the number 12 N 23/2/73/29. My thanks to Clare Lanigan for having brought this valuable document to my attention.
6. Royal Irish Academy 12 N 23/2/73/29.

13

THE CROSS OF CONG

The Cross of Cong has recently been described by Griffin Murray[1] as 'the most important reliquary surviving from early medieval Ircland' and 'a *tour-de-force* of early medieval metalwork'. One of the inscriptions on it says, in so many words, that it contained a piece of the cross on which Christ was crucified, and so it is no wonder that its decoration is of the highest quality. The reliquary in the shape of a cross was made at the behest of Turlough O Conor, king of Connacht, in the 1120s, and was given to the Royal Irish Academy in 1839 by James McCullagh, who wrote a paper on it in the *Proceedings of the Royal Irish Academy* in 1838–9.[2] The next person to devote attention to it was George Petrie, who provided a reading of the various inscriptions in a paper in the same *Proceedings* for 1847–50.[3] The Royal Irish Academy preserves a letter[4] written by O'Neill from 19 College Street, Belfast, on 22 October 1855, to James Graves, Honorary Secretary of the Kilkenny and South-East of Ireland Archaeological Society at the time, giving his version of the inscriptions taken from his own rubbings. O'Neill points out how his version differs from Petrie's, and concludes that the letters of the inscription were not made by punches but were sunk.

Sixteen days later, on 7 November, O'Neill announced publicly[5] his observations on the inscriptions, in which he sharply criticised Petrie on five counts, including the introduction of spaces between words and full stops where none existed, and the addition of 30 letters and the subtraction of one; he also noted a few other errors made by Petrie, among them the omission of contracting signs over certain words. At a meeting of the Society on the following 19 March, the famed Kilkenny-born scholar John O'Donovan took up the cudgels on Petrie's behalf,[6]

pointing out that Petrie's version was hurriedly prepared, written in a popular style, and was a reading rather than a facsimile of the inscriptions; that it had been properly read by Petrie before the cross was removed to Dublin; and that it had been given in O'Donovan's own *Irish grammar* of 1845.[7] O'Donovan pointed out that the lack of contraction signs which O'Neill had complained about was explained by the fact that, in his reading, Petrie had expanded the contractions correctly, thereby creating the extra 30 letters. O'Neill's criticisms of Petrie were described by O'Donovan as 'puerile', being 'truly disgraceful to enlightened scholars, and sincere enquirers after truth'. Nevertheless, O'Neill was able to write to Windele from London on 21 March, saying that 'everyone who has written to me about the Cong paper expresses himself, as you do, much pleased',[8] and got the Dublin printer O'Daly to reissue his paper in a private printing.

In the previous October O'Neill had written to O'Donovan,[9] asking him to recommend the *High crosses* book to people; after O'Donovan's paper of March 1856 referred to above, however, he need not have expected any further helpful response, nor did he probably get any after his next diatribe against O'Donovan. In a response, again printed by O'Daly (on a single sheet),[10] he castigated O'Donovan for supporting his friend Petrie when O'Neill believed that he (O'Neill) had 'truth on his side, and that Dr O'Donovan is battling on the side of error', insisting that he, and not Petrie, had the correct reading of the inscription. In a much later letter to Sir John Gilbert (see quotation on pp 54–5), O'Neill expressed regret that people were accusing him of getting down to a personal level of attack, which he felt was unfair; this last response to

Fig. 42—'*The Royal Cross of Cong*', a print of 1879 which was O'Neill's last published work. Reproduced by courtesy of the National Library of Ireland (PD 4154 TD).

THE ROYAL CROSS OF CONG.

O'Donovan, however, of which a copy is preserved in the Royal Irish Academy, is little more than personal invective against both Petrie and O'Donovan, though O'Neill would have thought that the dispute was being conducted at a purely academic level.

Further comments later in the century by Petrie's collaborator and posthumous editor Margaret Stokes—both in her edition of Petrie's *Christian inscriptions in the Irish language*[11] and her own privately printed paper *Notes on the Cross of Cong* (with coloured lithographs based on her own facsimile readings that she had prepared in 1860)—make absolutely no mention of O'Neill's censure or of his version of the inscriptions.

O'Neill himself came back to the cross near the end of his life. The *Irish Builder* of 1 April 1879 reports that O'Neill, 'if he can get sufficient encouragement', proposes to produce a print of the Cross of Cong, the full size of the original, and in its various colours. The price was to be four guineas, and he was looking for subscribers. Then, on 1 March of the following year, he announces in the same periodical that the print has been produced. It 'represents the principal front of the cross, the other side is richly decorated, but in somewhat bolder style. The true art lover, the collector, or those who can afford the cost, should secure a copy of this beautiful and valuable print'— a copy of which is preserved in the National Museum in Collins Barracks, and another in the National Library (Fig. 42). This was O'Neill's last work. Ten months later he was dead.

NOTES

1. Griffin Murray, 'The Cross of Cong and some aspects of goldsmithing in pre-Norman Ireland', *Historical Metallurgy* **40** (1) (2006), 49.

2. Professor McCullagh, 'Account of the Cross of Cong', *Proceedings of the Royal Irish Academy* **1** (1838–9), 326–9.

3. George Petrie, 'An account of the Cross of Cong', *Proceedings of the Royal Irish Academy* **4** (1847–50), 572–85.

4. Royal Irish Academy 24 O 39/JG/114 (x).

5. O'Neill, 'Observations on the true reading of the inscriptions to be found on the Cross of Cong', *Proceedings and Transactions of the Kilkenny and South-East of Ireland Archaeological Society* **3** (1854–5), 417–19.

6. John O'Donovan, 'Observations relative to Mr O'Neill's observations on Dr Petrie's version of the inscriptions on the Cross of Cong', *Journal of the Kilkenny and South-East of Ireland Archaeological Society* **4** (1856–7), 37–40.

7. John O'Donovan, *A grammar of the Irish language published for the use of the senior classes in the College of St Columba* (Dublin, 1845), 228 and 234.

8. Royal Irish Academy 4/B/16/32.

9. Royal Irish Academy 24 O 39/JOD/299; written from an address at 19 College Street, Belfast, 15 October 1855.

10. A copy of this is preserved in the Royal Irish Academy, AP 1856/9.

11. George Petrie, *Christian inscriptions in the Irish language* (ed. M. Stokes), Vol. II (Dublin, 1878), 120–2 with pl. XLVIII, fig. 103 and pl. XLVIIIa.

Fig. 43—Photograph of Henry O'Neill holding a copy of *Ireland for the Irish* of 1868. The photograph may have been taken by his second wife, Juliet, and is preserved in Glenstal's 'Antiquities' folio.

14

LATER LIFE AND LEGACY

Henry O'Neill lived for four score years, having been born probably in the year of the Rebellion of 1798. As author of *Ireland for the Irish*, he was probably both gladdened and saddened to have lived long enough to see the height of the Land War, associated with evictions and names like Parnell, Davitt—and Captain Boycott. His strongly nationalist stance went back to the 1840s, when he joined the Repeal Association and painted watercolours of O'Connell and others, together with their luxurious prison apartments when they were imprisoned in the summer of 1844. It was also at that stage that he was criticised in the *Art Journal* for writing letters to a Dublin newspaper complaining about the Art Society's purchase of pictures by English painters. His argumentative nature flowed over into criticism of his arch-rival in the round tower controversy, George Petrie, and other members of the Royal Irish Academy with whom he disagreed, and his vehemence sometimes reached the verge of intolerance when it came to other people's views. He believed that 'the truth will out' in favour of his own opinions but, particularly in the case of the round towers, posterity has rightly discredited them.

Like Stanislaus, the father of his younger contemporary, James Joyce, he was always on the move. His surviving letters and the addresses he gave when exhibiting at the Royal Hibernian Academy and elsewhere show him constantly changing his abode, in one instance telling his friend John Windele that he was having a row with his landlord for not having paid a year's rent of twenty guineas.[1] This peripatetic existence, probably dictated by lack of money, can't have been too easy for his wife—or wives, for Strickland tells us that his widow was his second wife. This was Juliet, whom we have already met writing a letter to

Sir John Gilbert and who exhibited many of his paintings after her husband's death in order to help provide for their children. She was more than 30 years his junior for, in that letter to Sir John, she mentioned in 1897 that she was 66. We know nothing of O'Neill's first wife, who was probably the mother of the son Thomas mentioned in the Introduction (p. vii), but it is unlikely that she was the mother of a four-year-old son whom O'Neill reports in a letter to Windele[2] as having died in 1863. Through County Louth's distinguished historian Noel Ross, I have learned that the birth register in the Protestant church of St Nicholas in Dundalk records the baptism of three further children, Louisa O'Neill (born 8 January 1866), Pauline (born 30 May 1867) and Tyrone (born 1 June 1869). In each case the mother's name was given as Juliet, O'Neill's second wife, and it is remarkable that he was already in his late 60s when the first of these children came into the world, and over 70 when the last of them was born. We know also of a kind thought that he had for another boy, not his own, who was mentioned in a newspaper that Windele sent to O'Neill at around the time he was preparing his observations on the Cross of Cong inscriptions. O'Neill then replied to Windele in a letter from Belfast on 1 November 1855,[3] thanking him for his

> account of a poor ragged boy aged about 14 who acted as interpreter for a Greek sailor in a case brought before the Mayor [of Cork] charging the sailor's captain with cruelty. The boy appeared to be a master of Greek, German, Italian and Spanish. It is a pity that someone with such aptitude for the acquisition of languages should be left in his present position. I can't

do anything because I am too poor, but perhaps the people of Cork could help to give him a proper education.

In the same letter in which he reported on the death of his own little boy, O'Neill told Windele that he had 'set up a photo gallery for Mrs O'Neill at 32 Lower Sackville Street' [now O'Connell Street in Dublin], and Noel Ross kindly wrote to inform me that the *Dundalk Herald* of 22 August 1868 carried an advertisement for Mrs O'Neill's Photographic Gallery in Francis Street in the town. It was presumably she, then, who took the fine portrait photo of O'Neill (Fig. 43) preserved in the large 'Antiques' folio in Glenstal; this was taken no earlier than 1868, as it shows him holding on his lap a copy of *Ireland for the Irish*, which was published that year.

In her 1897 letter to Sir John Gilbert, mentioned above, Juliet gives her address as Fulham in London, where she went probably some years after her husband's death, but she must have kept up her connections with Ireland, as some one there must have informed her about Gilbert's remarks in the *Freeman's Journal*. What is surprising is that O'Neill states in *Ireland for the Irish* (p. 53) that he spent fourteen years of his life in England but, other than his catastrophic enlistment in the British army in the later 1840s and his time in London spent preparing his *Crosses* book, we know virtually nothing of his doings in England—apart, that is, from his *Guide to pictorial art*, published there in 1846.

All the bad press that O'Neill got from the Dublin archaeological establishment in his day did his subsequent reputation no favours, but we must counterbalance that with an appreciation of his not-inconsiderable achievements. Inspection of the sketch-books held in Glenstal will convince even the most sceptical that he was a very good sketcher of castles in particular, and it is a source of much regret to realise that he could have produced the first great book on Irish castles had he but started early enough to do so rather than leaving it until he was in his 70s, when he no longer had the strength to complete the task of assembling for publication the material he had collected for it over three or four decades. O'Neill has done us a great service in illustrating those castles which have since been demolished or which are now much less well preserved than they were during the third quarter of the nineteenth century.

His antiquarian artistry comes out at its best in the work for which O'Neill will forever be remembered and revered, his book on the *Sculptured crosses of Ireland*. This was a major undertaking for one man, as it represents not only his own very careful recording of those monuments whose international significance he was the first to appreciate but also a remarkable achievement in doing all the lithographs himself at such a large scale (22in. by 15in.), though it must have almost bankrupted him in the process. In his letterpress commentary on the 36 imperial folio plates, he was also the first to provide a reasonably comprehensive interpretation of the biblical scenes carved on the crosses, while at the same time being wise enough to admit that there were some which he was unable to interpret satisfactorily. It was in that great publication that he was at his best, combining his dual role as artist and antiquarian, though his illustrations for his *Fine arts* book of 1863 came a close second. In O'Neill's appeal for alms in the penultimate year of his life (see Chapter 12), he stated openly that his volume on high crosses was responsible for changing the shape and style of grave memorials from urns and other classical motifs to the ringed, so-called 'Celtic cross' which has proliferated in our cemeteries ever since, a point also well appreciated by Oscar Wilde. For the average citizen today, that is probably O'Neill's most lasting achievement, though, sadly, scarcely anyone nowadays appreciates his role in how that change came about.

His value as an artist rather than an antiquarian has never been sufficiently recognised, however—partly because many of his sketches remained hidden in the little-known sketch-books now fortunately preserved in Glenstal Abbey but also, more particularly, because his paintings are very poorly represented in public collections, both in Ireland and abroad. From the listings which Ann M. Stewart has compiled of the more than 100 original works (mainly watercolours) which O'Neill exhibited at various locations during his lifetime, and which his wife offered for sale after his death, we come to the stark realisation that only a tiny percentage are preserved in state institutions: three in the National Gallery of Ireland, and one each in the National Library and the Ulster Museum and Art Gallery in Belfast. Henry McDowell has probably the largest private collection of O'Neill's paintings, which make a remarkable contribution to the illustrations of this volume and which are, indeed, the catalyst for its production. Michael and Marianne Gorman, Cróine Magan, the Hon. Garech Browne, the earl of Erne and Dolores Treacy may also be counted among the private owners. Those not yet traced were sold by Sotheby's at Slane Castle in 1981, and by the Ivey-Selkirk Gallery in St Louis, Missouri, in 2007. But where have the others all gone? Now unrecognised or—perish the thought—destroyed? It is to be hoped that the appearance of this volume might make the present whereabouts of many more known, thereby helping to reinforce O'Neill's important place of honour in the art of the Victorian period in Ireland.

When O'Neill decided to go ahead with his *Crosses* book, he said himself that he was giving up his lucrative practice as a portrait painter, a talent which we see not so much through originals (of which scarcely any are preserved) but through his drawings of Young Irelanders as lithographed by Gluckman, copies of which are preserved in the National Library. All too little known is the remarkable series of his watercolours depicting the Richmond Bridewell when O'Connell and a small band of his closest associates were incarcerated there in 1844. These provide a dramatic backdrop to one of the most remarkable incidents in the Liberator's life, and one which helped him to cement his reputation outside Ireland. Let us hope that O'Neill's links with O'Connell and with Oscar Wilde, which form a bridge spanning decades of O'Neill's life, will help to augment the artist's reputation both inside Ireland and beyond.

In O'Neill's obituary, published in the 1 January issue of the *Irish Builder*, we read:

His efforts to vindicate Irish art, and the expenditure of his time and money on his literary undertakings, did not meet with that amount of response at the hands of his countrymen that he might have well anticipated if the true *amor patriae* moved them ... No doubt he estranged some who would have proven his friends, but the man's fixity of purpose and the tenacity with which he clung to his views, coupled with his great merit, were sufficient to wipe out his faults.

The obituary ends with a letter from J. Bernard Burke, Ulster King at Arms, pointing out that O'Neill's great work, *The sculptured crosses of ancient Ireland*, remains an enduring memorial of his industry and genius, and requesting contributions to help relieve the financial circumstances of the artist's widow, who was left impoverished after his years of straitened circumstances and oft-recurring illness—because Irish art is no gainful profession.

NOTES
1. Written from Church Place, Fermoy, on 1 September 1859; Royal Irish Academy 4/B/19/71(1).
2. Royal Irish Academy 4 B 23/20.
3. Royal Irish Academy 4A /B/15/81(1); written from 19 College Street, Belfast, on 1 November 1855.

APPENDIX

WORKS BY HENRY O'NEILL EXHIBITED

Ann M. Stewart did the art historical community a great service in publishing two sets of catalogues of exhibitions: *The Royal Hibernian Academy of Arts, index of exhibitors and their works 1826–1979* (Manton Publishing, Dublin, 1987), and *Irish art loan exhibitions 1765–1927* (St Ouen, Jersey/Dublin, 1995).

The following are extracts from her publications concerning Henry O'Neill (wc = watercolour).

ROYAL HIBERNIAN ACADEMY OF ARTS

2 Harry Street, Dublin
1835   A Scene near Lough Dan, Co. Wicklow, wc
Lough Bray, Co. Wicklow, wc
View of the Seven Churches, Glendalough, Co. Wicklow, wc
A distant view of Bray Head, wc
The round tower, Clondalkin, Co. Dublin, wc
Cabins at Clondalkin, Co. Dublin, wc
Annamoe, Co. Wicklow, wc
Sunrise at Luggelaw, County of Wicklow, wc

1836   Luggelaw, County of Wicklow, wc
Portrait of John Barton, Esq., wc
Dublin from the mountain side, wc
Lough Dan, County of Wicklow, wc
Waterfall in the Devil's Glen, County of Wicklow, wc

1837   Glenmore Castle, County of Wicklow, wc

The ruins of the arcade, as they appeared on Thursday, April 27, taken from Mr Sparke's Carpet Ware-house, Suffolk Street, wc [See William Laffan (ed.), *Painting Ireland* (Tralee, 2006), 196, fig. 1.]
Portrait of R. Graves, Esq., M.D., wc
Portrait of R. Graves, Esq., M.D., wc

39 Great Brunswick Street, Dublin
1838   South-west view of the Cathedral of Christ's Church, wc
Luggelaw, Co. Wicklow, wc
Mademoiselle Shieroni, as Amina, in the opera of La Sonnambula, wc
Portrait of a gentleman and his granddaughter, wc
A student, wc

North Earl Street
1840   Luggelaw, County of Wicklow, wc
Portrait of Mrs William Garbois, wc
Portrait of Mr Dawson, as O'Ruark, Prince of Breffni, in the new historical tragedy called 'Dermot McMurrough, or the Invasion' by the author of 'Jephtha's Vow': 'By the eternal majesty of heaven, I'll hunt him through the world 'till he shall swear its very width but makes it more unsheltering', wc
Portrait of Horatio Nelson, Esq., wc (but see p. 30)
Portrait of a young lady in a fancy costume 'Betty—"Oh, Liberta gradita"', wc
Portrait of a gentleman, wc
The African Roscuis, wc

Trinity College, Dublin

1841   An Irish farmer's cottage, county of Dublin—north side, wc
       Cleglin Castle, County of Meath, wc
       Beltard Castle, Co. of Clare, wc
       View near Rockbrook, County of Dublin, wc
       Puck's Castle, County of Dublin, wc

5 St Andrew's Street, Dublin

1842   Lough Bray, County of Wicklow, wc
       The round tower at Clondalkin, County of Dublin, wc
       The mountain side, wc
       View from Dalkey Rocks, looking towards Kingstown, County of Dublin, wc

1843   The pride of the valley
       Gandsey, the Killarney minstrel

1844   Castle Gar, Lough Corrib, County of Galway, wc

Ruthland, Grand Canal

1847   An evening scene
       Mid-day
       Near Shanganagh, County of Dublin, wc
       Robs Walls Castle—Malahide, wc
       Near Crumlin—County of Dublin, wc
       On the Shannon, near Portumna, wc

1856   A wood, wc

Church Place, Fermoy

1859   The Blackwater, near Fermoy
       £40 0 0
       Brian Boru's Castle, Ballincollig, Co. Cork
       £20 0 0

1860   Blarney Castle, Co. Cork
       £21 0 0
       Near the Blackwater, below Fermoy
       £10 0 0

Castle Inch(y), on the Lee
£12 0 0

Frances Street, Dundalk

1871   The battlefield of Faughart, north side of Dundalk
       £10 0 0
       Hugh O'Neill's Castle—Co. Tyrone
       £10 0 0
       Roche's Castle—four miles west of Dundalk
       £3 0 0
       A mountain cliff on the north side of Dundalk
       £7 0 0
       Badgers
       £7 0 0
       Dunmahon Castle, Co. Louth
       £5 0 0
       Rural companions
       £7 0 0
       A stranded boat
       £1 10 0
       Kilsaran or Greenmount
       £ 3 0 0

1872   Milking time★
       £21 0 0
       The song of the lark★
       £63 0 0
       Sheep
       £5 5 0
       The mountaineers★
       £25 0 0

1873   An Irishman carrying his pike in a proclaimed district
       Ancient castle in Maudlin Street, Kilkenny

109 Lower Gardiner Street

1874   Portrait of the Rev. Thaddeus O'Malley
1875   Portrait of Prof. Glover
1876   Ormond Castle, Kilkenny (National Gallery No. 1919?)

1879   The worn-out donkey

*Because of the suddenly higher prices, there is a possibility that the items marked with an asterisk may have been by Henry O'Neil, whose prices are generally higher.

DUBLIN EXHIBITION OF ARTS, INDUSTRIES, MANUFACTURES & LOAN MUSEUM

1872   The successful launch   £21 0 0
       Lent by Henry O'Neill
       Castle Roche, near Dundalk, wc   £5 0 0
       Ditto
       Glasdrummond Lough, Co. Armagh   £5 0 0
       Ditto
       The fern gatherer—scene on the County Louth mountains, wc
       Ditto

IRISH   EXHIBITION   OF   ARTS   AND MANUFACTURES, DUBLIN

1882   View of Blarney Castle—sunset   £10 10 0
       Lent by Mrs Juliet O'Neill
       Ruins of abbey, Co. Louth   £8 8 0
       Ditto
       View of Glendalough—evening   £10 10 0
       Ditto
       Landscape water colours, the round [tower] and St
       Canice's Cathedral, Kilkenny   £8 8 0
       Ditto
       Group of sheep   £5 5 0
       Ditto

109 Lower Gardiner Street
       Water colour drawing   £7 7 0
       View of stone-roofed architecture at Gallarus, Co.
       Kerry   £10 10 0

Ditto
Ruins of the Franciscan Abbey, Drogheda
(morning)   £8 8 0
Ditto
View of Glendalough—sunset   £10 10 0
Ditto
Ruins of castle at Trim   £8 8 0
Ditto
Portrait of Mrs O'Neill
View of ruins of Howth Abbey   £8 8 0
Ditto
Landscape and cattle, Fermoy, Co. Cork
                                                       £5 5 0
Ditto
Rev. Thaddeus O'Malley, author of 'Home Rule on
the Basis of Federalism'   £16 16 0
Ditto
Marine view, Killiney   £6 6 0
Ditto
Landscape at Roundwood, Co. Wicklow—thatched
cottage and farm haggard   £6 6 0
Ditto
Portrait of Rev. J. O'Hanlon
Ditto
Landscape—Blarney Castle   £26 5 0
Ditto
Water-colour landscape and castle—companion
                                                       £7 7 0
Ditto
Study of beech trees—taken at Fermoy, Co. Cork
                                                       £5 5 0
Ditto
Ruins of Franciscan Abbey, Drogheda (evening)
                                                       £8 8 0
Ditto
Julia's pet   £6 6 0
Ditto
Water-colour, landscape and castle (companion)
                                                       £7 7 0
Ditto
A mountain scene—rainbow

Ditto

Rustic sketch

Ditto

Landscape—round tower at Lusk, Co. Dublin

£6 6 0

Ditto

Landscape at Roundwood, Co. Wicklow

Ditto

Ruins of Adair Abbey   £7 7 0

Ditto

Landscape view of the round tower at Clondalkin

£6 6 0

Ditto

CORK INDUSTRIAL EXHIBITION

1883 A group of sheep   £7 7 0

Blarney Castle   *For sale*

Ditto

Blarney Castle   *For sale*

Ditto

Glendalough   *For sale*

Ditto

View of Glendalough—sunset, wc   £10 10 10

Round tower and church, wc   £21 0 0

Landscape with cattle   *For sale*

The meeting of Essex and Tyrconnell at the ford

For sale

IRISH EXHIBITION IN LONDON

1888 Blarney Castle

Ditto

A National School girl, wc

Ditto

Howth Abbey, Co. Dublin, wc

Ditto

The Yellow Tower, Trim, wc

Ditto

Meury [Moyry] Pass and Castle, Co. Louth, wc

Ditto

St Laurence Gate, Drogheda, wc

Ditto

Portrait of the artist, wc

Ditto

Mountain sheep, a study, wc

Ditto

Clondalkin round tower, wc

Ditto

Sheep, a study in oil

Lent by William A. Hinch

Pass of Moira, wc

Ditto

Corn stooks

Ditto

Portrait of the artist

Ditto

CORK INTERNATIONAL EXHIBITION

1902 The first born

Lent by Lady Russell of Killowen

GUILDHALL EXHIBITION OF WORKS BY IRISH PAINTERS, LONDON

1904 The first born

Lent by Lady Russell of Killowen

IRISH INTERNATIONAL EXHIBITION, LONDON

1907 The Cave of Dunmore, Co. Kilkenny

Lent by John Campbell Nairn

A sheep, wc

Lent by Dr Canon Travers Smith

Head of a calf

Ditto

WHITECHAPEL EXHIBITION OF IRISH ART, LONDON

1913   Cave of Dunmore, Co. Kilkenny
        Lent by John Campbell Nairn
        Portrait of a man
        Lent by Gerald Wakeman
        The first born
        Lent by Lady Russell of Killowen

LOAN EXHIBITION OF PAINTINGS, BELFAST

1921   Study of a head, wc
        Lent by E.G.S. Stringer

INDEX